The
SPLENDID WAYFARING

BY

HALDANE MACFALL

With a Preface by Frank Brangwyn
and a personal note by Gordon Craig

1930
WALTER V. McKEE
INCORPORATED
NEW YORK

MANUFACTURED IN THE UNITED STATES OF AMERICA
BY THE VAIL-BALLOU PRESS, INC., BINGHAMTON, N. Y.

TO

HIS ROYAL HIGHNESS
THE CROWN PRINCE OF SWEDEN

HOMAGE

H. M.

CONTENTS

A NEW PREFACE

BY

FRANK BRANGWYN

Although I am not much of a hand with the pen, I should like to take this opportunity to say something about the man who knew all about art and artists. Haldane Macfall's warm heart always led him to see the best and to use his pen to help those artists whose works he loved to praise.

In this work Haldane Macfall has got down to the basic fundamentals of all art and interpreted the appreciation of art so that all who read may understand it. Here is no dishing up of hackneyed laws and recipes but an actual delving into the foundations of Art itself.

All Arts are akin; and Haldane Macfall realized this vital fact. There has been too much intellectual dishonesty in so-called criticism, academic wading in the quagmire of Aesthetics. Haldane Macfall found all the bookish theories to be dead stuff; he went straight to life, came to grips with life, and discovered that living art is only to be found in the interpretation of Life—in the personal expression of the impression that life made upon the creative artists. That, it seems to me, is the foundation of the whole thing; and that is what he here stated it to be.

The whole field of the emotions is the realm of Art—it is high above the field of the intellect—all the supreme acts of man are impelled by the emotions, not by the reasoned intellect. Most of the quarrels of the schools of criticism are due to the confusion of craftmanship with Art. The artist has to go through a mighty labor of craftmanship before the hand answers at will to the brain. The critics get lost by mistaking the craft of the fingers for the impression or the moods that, however blundering our hands, we try to arouse in our fellowmen by our art.

Haldane Macfall did not dogmatize or misunderstand this essential point. I was overjoyed to find this man stepping out of his own art of literature, and understanding the motives that the artists have given, and are giving, their lives and careers to create, instead of trying to shackle the feet of the artist with cast-iron laws that artists do not understand.

The critics can only receive the artist's revelation like any other human being, but they proceed to try to dictate to it various laws of the reason which have no meaning to the senses. Haldane Macfall realized that the only value of criticism is to appreciate art whenever found, and in this book he tries to lead his fellowmen to it. No law of criticism founded on logic is of any value. Nothing more proves this futility of philosophy or reason trying to set limitations on Art than the widely accepted futility that Art is Beauty. Art is a far more vast empire than beauty—Art is concerned with ugly and horrible emotions, with tragedy and with hideous emotions as much as with beautiful and tender emotions, and to make ugliness, or horrible or hideous emotions appear beautiful is to commit the foulest sin in art. Through Art the human may know the widest gambit of emotions at second hand —and through Art only.

It is through the emotions, above all through the emotions arising to heroic force in the passions that man achieves his highest self—just as, deserting the nobler passions and giving himself up to baser passions he realizes his baser self.

No artist works, or has worked on bookish systems. No master drags out a canvas and says: By thunder! I'll achieve the Pyramidal! Here goes for Unity, inspired by Vitality, brushed in with Infinity, and qualified by Repose. This is all very well if you are trying to teach a student to become an artist in twelve lessons. I do not say that no man so paints; for one sees work at times that could have been created in no other way. But it is not the way of the masters, it is the way of the school-masters. The methods and aims of an artist are deeper and more profound; they are beyond the reach of explanation and all recipe.

There is one note in particular in this book that is sounded again and again and it is that the artist can only achieve vital art by uttering himself. The moment he tries to mimic others his art is debauched, his creation withers, however much his craftmanship may gain. The moment that a painter becomes a mimic, and only strives to repeat what has already been said with unmatchable skill, he becomes an imitator, and ceases to be an artist. Mimicry has always killed all utterances of a people in art. Personality is the supreme triumph of an artist.

Here is a book in which the writer does not befog Art in a mass of words about Aesthetics and Laws

of Style. Haldane Macfall gives the reader the key
to an appreciation of Art. From him one learns that
art is not religion or lack of religion—it is not
morals or lack of morals—it is the emotional com-
munism of man with man. It is nothing else, but
it is all that. And being that, it is a colossal significance. Without art, without means to become partakers in the experience of our fellowmen at second
hand, we should live little above the brutes, things
of little moment. We can know the sorrows of the
disconsolate and the triumph of the great—all life
lies an open book to us.

I feel that Haldane Macfall has done more in this
book than any other writer before to put into
words these vital facts. It is a fine achievement.

A PERSONAL NOTE ON
HALDANE MACFALL
BY
GORDON CRAIG

HALDANE MACFALL was the most generous of
men and he gave in the most extravagant way that
a man can give for he gave his time and his talents
to others. Gifted as a writer and as a draughtsman,
he gave time from these two gifts of his—he gave I
think a third of that time. He worked hard but
never so passionately as when it was to write upon
the work of someone else. And to write of that was
to praise. I do not think a fresher laurel ever sprang
from that tree from which we pluck those leaves to
make dry wreaths of victory. Dear Macfall's
wreath is fresh and living.

It was this way. While writing his novels or his-
tories, he would suddenly chance to see some little
wood engraving or drawing by some beginner with
some talent or promise in it. To this (even to its
lack of fulfillment) he, the good fellow, would respond—leave his writing—go out and find the

artist, talk big, talk merrily—rage against the times
which ignored great art, blaze a bit—always heart-
ily—and finally, going away with three or four
prints or designs, or even ten, would write an article that same day to tell the world how he had discovered a genius. He would come out with super-
latives in praise of this "genius" (I was one of them
so I know) and he would get the article accepted
and printed and thus we would all feel cheered up.
Life seemed easier for a while and for some of us
actually became easier if the Macfall article hap-
pened to catch the right eye. For then we actually
sold something.

Who reads this? The artist? One of you who sold
but little? Then you know it's true and you know
what 10 pounds meant to us in those days. It seems
to me that I only voice but feebly the big shout of
gratitude which goes up to Macfall (some years too
late perhaps) from all our hearts. From Brangwyn
down to Lovat Fraser, dozens benefited by the
staunch and appreciative articles which "Old
Mac", as he was called by those men who loved
him, was always prone to pass off into the press, in-
sisting that the journal should publish his praise.
Some don't insist you know.

Besides this elemental goodness of his, he was greatly talented—and when I read *Jezebel Pettyfer,* in 1898 (I think it was that year) I thought it a very fine novel. To-day it is at last being praised. His *History of Painting,* a work in eight volumes, cannot be as good as his novel, because here he was not in his creative sphere. But it is so much better than those dry books of fifteen volumes which learned and less delightful people bring out. Then came *The Masterfolk* and *The Splendid Wayfaring* —to sound a full peal on the bells he was ever so ready to ring for life and art, so that they might be heard by the whole village. To me, whenever I heard them afar off, all they said was "Hal-dane-Mac-fall" and all I could call back was, "Bless him".

But to many others they meant a very great deal. He was like the bells he played on—a good exaggeration. He detested tinkling. He waxed wroth (in a merry way) at the notion of being over careful not to exaggerate.

He had been in the English Army—that perhaps was something he gloried in more than in the arts or in the efforts of his friends. He was an emotional being yet he was still able to live in England and to love all that unemotional England stood for or kept him from.

Altogether he was one of the very best and some-one should write a record of his years as a soldier, as artist, and as student in Paris—in the days when Yvette Guilbert was a young girl and wore her long black gloves—and as the friend of young artists struggling to get on. The last part of the record would prove the most difficult because people are rather apt to forget benefits received—they forget them for they never quite realise them as they are bestowed upon them. But could they realise this I for one believe they would not fail to express the gratitude they'd immediately feel when remember-ing Haldane Macfall.

THE PERSONAL NOTE

TO all of us, who essay to create Art, the time comes when our intelligence cries out to us: What is this that we are trying to do? Is it worth the sacrifice of our whole life's endeavour? Is it so important a thing that we shall give to it the short span of our adventure here on earth—the all too swiftly sped years that are so precious to us; which are ours for all too brief a while; which once flown, can never again be ours? Is this awful isolation from the jigging, eager world outside, this laborious driving of the ink over reams of paper, this painting of messy, ill-smelling colours on canvas, this handling of wet clay, this making of music on catgut—is all this labour of such enormous value, when we might be out on life's highway across the face of the world a-merry-making or living vast acts and sensations? Are we getting any nearer to the living of life than the poor, misguided fool who grubs, day in, day out, to snatch but gold?

So, also, that moment came to me.

*Beginning in early manhood to essay the crea-
tion of Art, both in literature and painting, I was
soon struck, as probably most artists, in contem-
plative mood, are struck, by certain prominent
facts. To begin with, I found myself compelled to
create a thing for which I had no excuse or guidance in mere caculated Reason; and I noticed that
whilst everybody, who wrote on the Arts, talked
cant about Art being Beauty, and that I myself also
had got the platitude into my head, I was really
all the time not in the least concerned with Beauty
or Lack of Beauty—and what was even more sur-
prising, on careful survey of their words, I found
that neither were the great writers and painters
of the age! Well-primed in the best writings upon
the laws of Art, that men call Æsthetics, from
Aristotle to Ruskin, I noticed, whilst I created by
Instinct and little concerned with Beauty or Lack
of Beauty, that when critics and the like came to
look upon my work I immediately jumped into
their atmosphere and tried to induce them to think
that I had thought in terms of Beauty! I noticed
that every other artist did the same! that we were
all confederates in a sort of conspiracy in this*

Beauty Show. I noticed this fantastic jargon of a fantastic Lie to be a general pose. I wondered if Art could be just this colossal, laborious, clever Lie.

On every hand I found men writing what is called Criticism. I looked upon the men who wrote these things; I listened to some; I read many. I often found that they stood before works of Art wholly missing what was revealed to me; that they praised bad things and passed by powerful and exquisite things; and I was filled with wonder. Then I noticed that few, if any, of them all were greatly concerned with living Art, but were looking upon living Art through the spectacles of past Art. They tossed about the catchpenny—they flung about the gabble of the studios, the chatter of the desk, the platitudes of the dead so-called critics and philosophers throughout the ages. They looked upon Art as a clever affair, wrought in tune to a code of laws laid down by tradition—they called this code of laws Æsthetics. They judged the living by the dead! They were ghouls in the graveyard of dead Art—sucking the brains of dead giants or lesser men; and, by consequence, they sought only in the living what they tasted in the dead!

Now, the chiefest law of all their vague vapour-

ings was this ever-perplexing law that Art is Beauty.

Soon thereafter I was plagued by another ques-
tioning. Not only did I find myself compelled to
create these things for which I had no excuse or
guidance in mere Reason, but I early discovered
that every effort to create a work of Art at all
compelled me as its basic intention to try to reach
the intelligence of my fellows—*and that, too, not*
by a bald direct logical statement of brain—I did
not in fact trouble about the Reason at all—but by
forcing my impressions with such power as I could
master into their intelligence through the channel
of their senses, trusting to the sensitiveness of their
feelings to be quickened and roused and answer to
mine. What was more, I noticed that every master
had done and did the same—always strove to con-
quer and reach the intelligence of his fellows
through their sensing. They did it quite instinc-
tively, scarce knowing why—they had been im-
pelled to it irresistibly; and only when they so
conquered had they achieved great Art. Yet every
one who wrote about Art treated and tested the
artist's work, not in terms of sensing, but in terms
of Reason; argued about it as if it were a science;
made laws and limitations for it—seemed to argue

that it was irrevocably settled by some Supreme Being that Art was an effort of man to create Beauty. They set up this code of Laws for Art, which they called Æsthetics; and they treated it almost with as solemn reverence as if it had been Holy Writ! To question 'Aristotle were as though one whistled in church.

Still more extraordinary: the artists, instead of saying to the critic and the professor, "We know nothing about your theories and your laws and your Aim of Beauty, we only know that we are urged by instinct to create what we feel so as to stir the like feelings in others," whilst they chafe and fret and fling contempt at the critics and professors behind their backs, seemed to be afraid of being accounted rather vulgar fellows if they challenged their precious Æsthetics. And on every hand the artists argued with the critics and professors, in this judging of Art, in terms of Reason; accepted the professorial and philosophical and critical laws about Beauty and the rest of it; and— when their work was completed—tried to prove that such work fitted these laws of Beauty!

But who, asked I, are the authorities and demigods who settle these laws of Æsthetics? Whittled

*down, it soon appeared that there were certain little
groups of people who considered that they were
cultured and alone able to understand Art; that
Art was really only created for them, and that all
this vast activity of the studios and of writers,
painters, musicians, the theatre, was a vast beehive
to make honey to tickle their palates—that all other
people were more or less tasteless, and could not
really understand works of Art at all unless they,
the cultured ones, taught them what to admire!
It appeared above all that the Greeks, Aristotle and
other dead writers, had solved the problem once
and for all; and before the self-appointed Cultured
admitted a work of Art to be Art at all they had to
put on the spectacles of Aristotle and test them so
—or the spectacles of Ruskin—or some other
philosopher's glasses. They spoke of the Renaissance with particularly solemn mouth, though they
realised the Renaissance so little that they did not
know how much less even Dante and the men down
to the great initiators of the Renaissance knew of
Greek than does the ordinary undergraduate of
to-day. They even hold that great Art stopped with
the Renaissance, and fell with the Tenebrosi!*

Now, the curious part of this elaborate Æsthetic,

*around which great Societies have been formed
(and apart from the strange fact that some of the
greatest creators of the Arts have never read a
word of Aristotle and the rest of them), was that
these extremely cultured self-ordained lords of Art
were themselves almost wholly sterile in the Art
they usurped; whilst quite "uncultured" people
would burst into song and create mighty masterpieces! but the conceit and self-assurance of the
"Cultured" remained undimmed.*

   *But what exactly was this Art? The philosophers
gave me no answer. The critics gave me no answer. Each one solemnly contradicted the other;
all were simply rehashing bookish theories; none
of them were creating any particularly great Art
—but the more mediocre they were, the more dog-
matic they! I read the artists who had written
on their Art; I found them but special pleaders
for their own particular vision, nay, even more
for their own particular practice of craftsmanship
and their own achievement. I found both critics
and artists distorting the word Beauty, until Hen-
ley openly spoke of the "Beauty of Ugliness"!
What I did notice, however, that made a vast gulf
between artists and critics, was that artists, whilst*

they wrote one thing, when they practised their Art did another quite different thing—that, in fact, when they followed their instincts and the urging of their imagination to create impressions as their senses had felt them, they created Art— when they followed laws of Æsthetics and tried to make a work of Art on principles directed by Reason, they failed to create Art!

OF such strange stuff is this intellectual snobbery on which youth is nourished, and the wreath of honour woven for the judges of Art!

Now, for years, whilst critics and professors and philosophers and pedants have been writing upon Art, I have been collecting, filing, and weighing criticism. For this reason: About the time that I was a young cadet at Sandhurst, London town being convulsed with amusement at the ridiculous Art of a man called Whistler, and Academicians angry about it, I thought I would stroll into the London gallery where he held his display and have a laugh as loud as any. I found myself in the presence of so profound a revelation in painting that I looked round for the mockers, only to discover a score of silent men and women equally impressed. I realised, as at a stroke, that the writings of Ruskin, who could only see in this masterwork the "flinging of a pot of paint at a canvas by an impudent Cockney," were not only valueless as to all Art whatsoever, but that unless Ruskin had bookish authority for his judgments, he did not know a work of Art when he saw it! that the moment he stood face to face with living, pulsing Art he had not sufficient sensing of Art to understand its significance, or subtlety of sensing to receive its utterance. The revelation made a profound impression upon me.

From that moment I challenged all "authorities" on Art; only to find them all steeped in falsities, and their theories untenable. But it is easy to destroy a rotten thing. The trouble was to build. It was clear that the men who wrote on Art did not understand its significance. What was the basic significance of Art? Obviously all depended on that.

Well; I collected into a list the supreme works of Art in literature, whether verse or prose—in painting—in sculpture—in drama. This was no difficult affair, for I only took unassailable masterpieces. The next thing was to seek in them for that

*which was the vital essence and common signifi-
cance and intention of them all. Creation was common to all; to what end?*

*In weighing, rejecting, reducing, and sorting, I
found that whilst Art, like all that is intelligent
to the human, is addressed to the brain, it always
had to reach the understanding by a totally and
markedly different route than by the Reason; it
was soon further clear that it always, without exception, reached the brain by way of the senses—
it was addressed to our sensing, and only through
the alchemy of our senses did it, and could it, reach
and stir the intelligence. Clearly it was wholly apart
from Reason.*

*I had stood baffled before the Law that Art was
Beauty, and had Beauty as its aim; the which had,
from reiteration of the generations, become unconsciously part of my own thinking—or unthinking. I forthwith searched and weighed this thing
called Beauty that I had set on the altar of faith,
and found that it was a falsity—a sham. If not,
then some of the most powerful works of Art
wrought by man's skill must be accounted as
naught! At once the House of Lies came crashing*

down. And when the dust cleared away, where had been a tawdry Idol was a wondrous Light.

I had gone to the critics, the philosophers, the æsthetes; everywhere they had failed me. Not one, from Ancient Greece to the Victorian years, had set up a standard of Art that would measure more than a tithe of the masterpieces of Art—to employ the standard of any was to reject some of the mightiest of the masterpieces. Pleasure, Amusement, Praise, all failed as much as Beauty when applied as touchstone.

Once led to rebellion against all this tyranny of a false intellectual inquisition into Art, a remarkable fact loomed. Whilst the sole language of mere intellect was Speech; whilst intellect appealed to intellect in pure Reason by cold calculated and carefully weighed words of truth, the Arts, without exception, had this in common, that they had first deliberately to create and employ a Make-Believe before they could utter themselves. The Arts took a stone and shaped it to trick the intelligence by an illusion; took paint and painted make-believe things on walls or canvas to trick the intelligence by an illusion; the actor painted his face and dressed up and pretended to be some one else in order to trick the intelligence through an illusion; the playwright wrote words into the mouths of characters to trick the intelligence by an illusion—always a sham thing had first to be created. Clearly, then, Art was not an appeal to the intelligence through cold Reason. But the strange thing about it all was that this Make-Believe aroused the intelligence through the senses with a power and a compelling conviction that the cold Reason could not approach! And, strangest of all, it was only when this Make-Believe convinced the intelligence of the truth of the desired impression that the intelligence accepted it! In other words, the Make-Believe was valueless unless it suggested the truth; but once created as a truth, it passed into our experience as though we ourselves had experienced it.

Here was the basic foundation of Art being cleared. Reason and Art were two absolutely different means for the communion of the intelligence of man with man. The one was a direct statement from brain to brain; the other was a statement to the intelligence that had to reach it by way of the senses—and could reach it by no other way except through the senses.

Thereafter I took fearless, untrammelled Truth for a corner-stone, and built upon it; and as I built, the acreage of the garden of Art became vaster, and brought forth significance at every hand; and from a garden it grew into a kingdom; and from a kingdom into an immensity that reached to the stars— for it loomed large as life itself. Where had been a marble sepulchre on barren ground, littered with the traffic of the antique dealer and the waste-paper of empty scribblers, there came to view a living splendour.

To others who have been mute, perchance this revelation may also have been vouchsafed.

It was a heavy confirmation of these researches, that I began to utter in print in the early 'nineties, when Tolstoy, in giving forth "What is Art?" showed that he had been employed upon parallel lines of research. The keen and forthright vision and fearless courage of Tolstoy had also discovered the falsity of Art being Beauty; and he came near to discovering the whole basic significance; but, unfortunately, when he proceeded to apply his dis-

*coveries, he allowed what men call Religion to over-
whelm his judgment, and to turn him aside into
another wayfaring, confusing his sensing of the
full and just significance of Art, if in a noble conception of man's destiny. So that he, too, set up
another issue as the aim of Art, and came to judging works of Art in fantastic fashion. For Tolstoy,
Art was soon being compelled to array itself in the
religion of Tolstoy—to see with his eyes, to hear
with his ears—and the function of Art is far more
vast than to pander to any man's religion or want
of religion.*

*It has since come about that what I uttered in
fragments, masquerading under another name, has
been seized upon by others, avowedly or una-
vowedly, and been distorted and falsified or misunderstood. I therefore write these pages to re-state
a significance, to purify it, to utter it as I have
seen it, and to reaffirm my concept and my faith;
that thereby, perchance, it may bring some light
to youth, and be a lamp to draw back to the pursuit
of vital things those that stray in futile and aimless
wandering amidst the graveyards where the great
or lesser dead lie buried; and where no living
thing is.*

*What, then, is the basic significance of Art?
What is its ultimate intention? What is its essence
and its range?*

BEFORE *we can get even a shallow concept of the
basic significance of Art it is necessary to have some
rough idea of what we mean by Life. Let us take
a glance at what we know of Life so far as human
inquisition has been able to tear away the veil. To
do so needs that we put aside for a while religion
and morals, with which we are wont to prejudice
and befog our concept of Life at every turn, each
according to our tradition—for religion, when all's
said, from a work-a-day point of view, is the rough
and ready compromise between the general concept
of Conduct of an age on the one hand, and a vague
following, or rather intention to follow, the ideals
of some great Founder of conduct on the other.
For instance, white Western peoples affect Christianity; but they are torn with wrangles as to what
each man considers to be Christianity, whilst in
the bulk they set up a rude code of conduct
which is often wholly inimical to the basic ideals
of their Teacher. Let us take the business community, the trading mass of which is concerned from*

morning to night with profit by usury, with screw-
ing down one neighbour, to part with what he has
at the lowest price, so that Commerce may sell to
another neighbour at the highest price that it can
compel upon him, even starve him into. Here we
have the commerce of the people absolutely opposed to the ordering of the Christ, who bitterly
assailed usury and the getting the better of one's
neighbour—indeed, the Christ's only recorded act
of violence was the chastisement of the money-
changers! Again, armies are blessed as they go to
war under the banner of the Prince of Peace! And
so with all religions.

Morals, again, vary from generation to generation and from peoples to peoples.

Without prejudice to religion or morals, then,
let us set them aside for the moment, and try to
see what is known as Life by us to-day, rid of all
bias, so far as it can be known and accepted by all
civilised folk, whatever their nationality, creed, or
code.

FOREWORD

TO THE STUDENT, THE PROFESSOR, THE CRITIC AND THE MAN IN THE STREET

NOW, your ordinary man, what time he can spare from the fantastic business that he has set up as his "calling" or "object in life," gives a certain serious consideration in his day to phases of his mind which he calls "religion" or "recreation" or "culture" or "sport" or "getting on," or the like. His "religion," 'tis true, he keeps at solemn arm's length, shrinks from being on too familiar a footing with it, treats with aloof and reverential respect lest it overstep decorum, be guilty of familiarity, and enter too intimately into his conduct—though he compel it upon his neighbour with dogged resolution. His "recreation" he takes more whole-heartedly—or as whole-heartedly sees to it that his neighbours shall not take it, which is only another, if greyer, form of recreation. But the most vital faculty that is granted to him, whereby he alone may increase the splendour of life, he thrusts aside among the lesser things, accounting it of less significance in his day

than his sport—to say nothing of food and drink
and money.

Nay, the very word Art, which is the next most
important in his short wayfaring to Life itself, he
associates with a painting in a gilt frame by some
long-dead artist, which he does not understand, but
respects as a fetish because in some vague way he
realises that large sums of money are needed to pur-
chase it—by people who understand the art of it
perhaps as little as he. The Great, and the heirs to
the once Great, living in a palatial atmosphere, are
surounded by masterpieces of painting of antique
days—for which they care or do not care—and
they that are new come to wealth, being at their
wits' end, often as not, to know what to do with it,
and seeing that grandeur is handsomely housed and
that it is part of this handsomeness to be sur-
rounded by master-pieces of the days that are gone,
feverishly strive to load their new mansions with
these antique things, mistake this for Art and a love
for Art, do not know a vital work of Art of their
own age when they see it, create a traffic in the
works of the dead; and to this traffic pander
swarms of "experts" and "critics" and "professors
of Art" and the rest of it. Museums are set up and

are held to be an incentive to the creation of the Arts!

With Art as the critics and professors and philosophers understand it, I am not here greatly concerned; but wholly with Art in its stupendous and vital need for the peoples who would rise to the mastery of the world and know the fulness of life.

For I tell you that *Art is absolutely necessary to all civilised life, to all intelligent living—that is to say, all life outside a madhouse. It is with us from the cradle to the grave. We cannot escape it. Without Art we are back again on all fours, as when man made his habitation in the branches of the trees and cracked nuts to find his sustenance, and was little more than the beasts.*

Men follow after strange gods, and at the end of their little strut upon the stage, as the curtain rings down, they complain bitterly that life is a hollow thing! Aforetime they bowed to the god of war or bent knee to this thing or another that they set up as their ideal; to-day it is wealth. Men who have built or hoarded vast "fortunes" are solemnly interviewed for the envious, are accepted as great men, and affirm that money-getting is their chief incentive to life. God! what a tragedy for a people!

When all's said, and the worship done, a very vulgar dullard, if he give all his powers to it, can, and often does hoard great wealth—indeed, he is at times a criminal against society. But even the significance of *his* wayfaring for himself does not lie in his wealth nor in his lack of wealth—greatness is not wealth nor lack of wealth, whatever else it may be. The significance of a man for himself rests in the largeness of the range of his adventure in living; the significance of his wayfaring for others rests in the amount whereby he has increased the realm of life for his fellows.

We live a little mean day, so petty indeed that most men—honest fellows—deem themselves as having lived who go to their graves the narrow lifelong slaves of a paltry wage, content to have earned just that wage, as though earning a wage were life! nay, proud to be able to say as they lie a-dying that they have walked without tripping in a little parish. They are even acclaimed "good citizens"! But the largest and widest life is for him who dares the fullest adventure—who has become partaker in all that life can give. And by the Arts alone shall he know the fullest life; and by lack of the Arts shall he know the meanest.

The artist, in the full meaning of the word, is the supreme man.

It is well, therefore, to try and realise what is Art, and what is an artist.

THE SPLENDID WAYFARING

~~~~~~

Chapter I

OF LIFE

WHENCE Life comes, or whither it goes, these remain the eternal mystery; but that it is, and that it
has increased in fulness, we know—as sure as that
there is the firmament above us.

At the back of all, away in the myriads of years,
this wondrous thing that we call Life essayed from
the first to find a lamp in which its flame might
burn most brightly. Life sought to fulfil itself in
crystals. Baulked by the rigidity of rocks, it made
for itself a dwelling-place in the forms of plants;
baffled by plant forms that it created for its lamp
it dived into the ooze, at first attached to a spot,
slowly freeing its habitation into moving forms.
Baulked by the waters, it advanced from the fish
in the seas to the reptile that could move on sea or
land; and for æons, in forms of mighty reptiles, it
sought a wider fulfilment of itself. Baulked again,
it evolved for itself the forms that could fly in the
air; and from the great-winged pterodactyls it took
to itself the feathered flight of birds. Baulked again,

but in each endeavour finding ever fuller and
higher forms wherein to sense itself, it evolved for
itself the forms of animals, essayed fleetness of foot,
strength, bulk, ferocity; built for itself the lithe
forms of great cats, and essayed to fulfil itself in
the brutal and ruthless ferocity of the tiger and the
lion. Baulked again, Life turned and sought fuller
sensing in the agile bodies of apes; made for itself
increase of cunning of brain. At last, out of the
mystic ways, the eager Life that is at the core of
all existing things, evolving from stage to stage a
fitting habitation wherein to dwell—and, in order
further to fulfil itself, requiring first to create for
itself a newer and more perfect lamp wherein to
flame—on a day finds its supreme habitation in a
wondering creature that drops from its apelike
habits in the trees, and with ungainly straddle on
firm earth, takes its upright stand upon tentative
hind legs—falteringly, hesitatingly, ready to drop
on all fours at a stumble—bodying itself forth as
Man—the Thinking Thing.

LIFE'S cunning, with increase of Cunning, notes
the hand's use and the value of that wondrous
thumb that is on the hand—to grip, to throw, to

hold. That Cunning that is to become Reason in the blinking thing that thinks; that Thumb that, with the brain's Cunning for guidance, is to chip tools and weapons from the Flint, and give confidence to this naked, defenceless being, and lead him forth from his lair in the thicket and the cave out into the open strife which, for the body's sustenance and welfare, with pitfall and with gin, is to put to naught the lion's strength, the wolf's tooth, the wild boar's fury, so that Man shall wrap the skins of these about him against the frost's nipping cold, and use their hides to save his feet from wounds; that is to strike fire from the whirled wood and the chill flint to bring warmth to him in the chattering winter, and give rise to the potter's craft, whereby also the earth's metals shall yield their ductile strength to his further enfranchisement; that is to break the dog and oxen and the horse to his bidding and service, and to gather flocks and herds that he may roam the pastures of the world; and, the wander-years being done, that is to fashion the plough whereby he shall settle on the land and till the ruddy earth and gather in the harvest of her increase to his body's nourishment; that is to invent the distaff and the spinning wheel and the loom to the weaving of cloth and fabric; that is to achieve the making of the fisher's net; that is to bring the vast wide world tributary to him—the elements and the brutes, the valley and the plain, mountain and rock, the stream and the raging seas, so that the exquisite eye of Man shall see the stars a myriad leagues beyond the eagle's ken, his skill of transit make the swiftness of antelopes a sluggard's pace, his calculating hand to cage the strength of many horses in the machinery's intricacies. Life, the miracle, weaving miracles!

THESE things being so, what vast hopes lie in Man's forward adventure! If Life, building itself such a palace wherein to dwell, shall have reached thereto through the æons by its wayfaring from plant and insect and reptile and fish and fowl, through the brutes, to this so high estate, who shall be so dull a dolt as not to have vision of a more wondrous habitation that shall be Beyond-Man in the æons to come? Yet there be those of so narrow a vision that they would deny the wayfaring and deny the Beyond, thinking Man the supreme lamp, as each lamp in the making accounted itself, did it think at all, as the supreme lamp—indeed, each lamp, however small, was a miracle. But Life goes on—and it is the eternal impulse and striving and intention of Life, its mighty quest and its All, that it shall build ever towards the fullest adventure of self-experience. The worlds will roll on, and pass into dust—the years will pile themselves into eternity—but Life will be for ever. Its lamps are flung down, worn out, discarded when they can no longer hold the flame to light the wayfaring; but new lamps are wrought—and newer—newer. For Life must be fulfilled to a larger and more majestic purpose; and the wayfaring be ever towards higher heights.

NOW, mark this well! Life evolves, developing upwards, always towards a higher type, *that it may know increase of fulfilment, a larger sensing.* At the same time it does not wholly discard, but persists in, its earlier forms of lamp, the types degrading as they fall away from forward endeavour, even such as they may know in their own forms, and becoming subject to the higher types—or even dying out altogether if desperately assailed. And 'twere well to dwell on this; for, as sure as there is a to-morrow, so surely does that people that ceases

to fulfil what life holds for it, pass amongst the
slave-folk and become subject to master breeds, and
is thrust into the waste places of the earth. The
being that shrinks from fulfilment is discarded by
Life, which proceeds to create the higher lamp in
which to flame.

Mark well another fact—a most significant fact
—for these are obvious facts, not guessing! Man,
the thinking thing, from his lair in cave and
thicket, increased his strength in the closeknit
brotherhood of the clan. He foregathered to the
valley councils; thence further increased fellowship in the village, uniting his skill and strength
with the skill and strength of others, until he that
had the potter's skill bartered his skill with him that
had the warrior's skill in battle, and he that had
the builder's skill bartered with these and with him
that had the metal-worker's skill; and thus and so
the trades and crafts arose, to the mutual strength-
ening of the people; so power and increase of the
fulness of Life, passing from the wild fellow of
the cavern and the lake to the wandering tribe,
passed therefrom to the settled village, and from
them that lived their narrow day in villages to
them that foregathered within the stout walls of

the populous city—from the city to the State, that crumbled the city's walls, grown inadequate against the power of States; from the State to the mighty Commonweal of the race that is fenced about, to its uttermost frontiers, by the vast bulwarks of its daring spirits.

By consequence, as Life fulfils itself towards fuller power and experience in pushing forward to know fullest sensing, the simple intercourse of the naked lowering thing which, with low, frowning brow, brooded upon the but scant desires and the mean wants of his narrow cave, yielded a larger converse that demanded a fuller range of words at the valley's gatherings; speech that in turn acquired a fuller gamut in the village's debate; this in turn brought forth the richer communion of the orchestral city's multitudinous voice; which in time passed into the twilight of discarded things, giving birth to the wider accents of the State; until even the language of the State, grown parochial, fades and slowly dies, and in dying gives place to the deep, august, far-reaching communion of the Race.

WE are come, then, to this: that Life, in order to fulfil itself, has builded the body of man as its su-

preme lamp in which to flame; that life ever pushes
on, unceasingly, unwearyingly, towards the further
perfecting of such a lamp as shall permit it to
flame most fully. What form the Masterfolk that
are beyond shall take is hidden from us; but it is
written upon the wall for all to read that Life shall
know the fullest experience and will build a habitation wherein to dwell in fullest fashion—that Man
shall so strive that he shall give Life the fullest experience or must pass amongst the lesser breeds—
that there is no resting, no halting place—that it
is not for man to find mastery by looking back,
but by urging forward—that all backward striving
is but mimicry of the dead, and means death. The
book of Destiny is not written in the Past, but
must be torn from the Future by forward adventure.

*Now what is this prodigious and overwhelming
faculty whereby Man has been lifted above the
brutes and set in mastery over them?*

IT is clear that in evolving Man as its supreme
effort to bring forth the lamp in which to flame,
Life in Man has thereby arrived above the brutes
by some faculty that is denied to the brutes. It was

not by courage, since the brutes have as sublime courage as he; nor by strength, nor by bulk, nor by ferocity, nor by ruthlessness, nor the like, since such were granted to the brutes in abundance in common with man. Indeed, these attributes could be employed destructively to that Brotherhood which alone has led man from the savage and brought him to mastery over all created things. We have seen that man arose above the brutes by union, by nothing but union; as he will always rise by union and nothing but union. One faculty denied to the brutes and granted to man stands out clear and explicit: that faculty was *the power to commune with the intelligence of his fellows, and to become partakers in their intelligence.*

Obviously, then, this faculty of intelligent communion is the most important and significant factor in the onward and upward adventure of Man. *In what manner has it been granted to us so to commune with our fellows?*

On the answer depends our significance as men above the brutes—our significance as to whether we shall reach to further heights.

Chapter II

OF ART

WHATSOEVER his religion or course of life may be, man's supreme desire is to live. Joy and happiness lead to the fulfilment thereof; Pain turns us from transgression against it. The burnt child avoids the fire. All is sacrilege that mishandles the wondrous miracle.

The most vastly interesting thing to Man is Life.

It is his feverish search, during this his little span, from birth to death, to discover its significance; it is his hope beyond the grave—eternal life.

Cramp a people enough, deny them life enough, and at last, sullenly they turn, and, gazing out of eyes that see red, they spill blood like water so that they may find fuller life.

Be his ambitions, his passing desires, his utterances, his denials, his affirmations, his acts, what they may—at the back of all, permeating all, above all, dominating all, unless he be a madman or an idiot, man's supreme instinct is to live. Life is the right and heritage of every one of us.

Whence it comes, whither it goes, this life—these
are a part of the eternal mystery. But we can and
ought to experience all of life 'twixt its coming
and its going that our powers will grant to us.

NOW, *there are only two paths by which we may
arrive at this wonderful and miraculous adventure
that we call Life. Either we must each of us live
the whole of the adventures of life ourselves; or
we can experience life at second hand, through our
fellow-men by their communication to us of their
adventures.*

Every man, of course, must be born, grow to
manhood, know hunger and thirst, love, and die.
But it is abundantly clear that the thoughts, the
emotions—or feelings or sensations—of the life of
any single being, even if he be one of the greatest
of the great, cannot but be child's play when set
beside the vast experience and perceptions of the
lives of mankind. Our solitary personal adventures
and experiences in life, though we bestride the
world like a Napoleon, can at best be but a small
and parochial affair, when all's said, as against the
multitudinous experience of our generation. Shut

off from communion with our fellows, we walk
little better than a blind man's wandering in a
desert place.

Fortunately for the destiny of man, it has been
granted to us to be able to know of life, to experience life, at second hand through the communion of our fellows. In that, at once, we stand
arrayed in splendour, supreme above the brutes. It
is thereby that we have gained lordship over all
created things. It is thereby that man has increased
his capacity and his power—has widened his boun-
daries—and has achieved his fullest self. That power
of communion, next to life itself, was the greatest
gift and heritage of all.

Now we can only know of life at second hand
from our fellows in two ways: we can share their
Thoughts by the communication of their *Thoughts*
to us; and we can also become partakers in their
life at second hand by the communication to us of
their *Sensations*—of the things that they have *felt*.
In other words, intelligence can reach intelligence
by two means only—either by direct speech, the
direct statement of brain to brain; or by and
through the channel of the senses, through which

the intelligence receives and can alone receive the
impression of what another intelligence has sensed.

And the difference of direct and sensed communion is prodigious. It is not enough to *speak* of
life in order to experience it—that is an affair of
Reason, of Intellect speaking to Intellect, alone.
Before we can experience life we must be made to
sense it—to feel it. For instance, it is one thing to
tell a person that some one did a cruel thing: it is
a vastly different thing to make that person feel
the cruelty of it.

Now, just as the Thoughts of others can only
become our Thoughts through the communion of
Speech; so the Sensations of others can only be
communicated to us when they make us feel
through our senses what they have felt—either by
so skilful a use of colours that these arouse through
our sight the impression of what Another has felt
through his Vision by the craftsmanship of Painting; or by the subtle employment of sounds into
our Hearing so that we feel what Another has felt
through the craftsmanship of Music; or by his con-
juring up our emotions through the cunning craftsmanship of words, as in Oratory or Prose or Verse
or the Drama or Romance, or the like; so that we

actually experience Another's sensations as though
we ourselves had lived them, and the whole gamut
of joy or sorrow, anger or pity, awe or laughter,
heroism or cowardice, may be brought into our
existence. *This power of being able to transfer to
others* our *sensations by a skilful playing upon their
senses is Art.* We are, then, granted the power to
exchange our intelligence by two means: we can
exchange our Thoughts; and we can exchange our
Sensations. Speech is the means whereby we exchange our Thoughts—or, if you will, the means
whereby we exchange our Reason. But mere speech
cannot give us communion of the sensing of our
fellows. The means whereby we pour into the sensing of our fellow-men the impressions which have
been aroused in our senses so that we can enable
others to feel what we have felt—is the function of
Art; its whole function, and its only function.

The province of Art, then, is the wide realm of
the Imagination; it is born of the Imagination; is
rooted in the Imagination; grows in the Imagination; and blossoms and bears fruit in the Imagination—aroused through the senses.

The music pipes up a dancing measure—trips it
in merry fashion, gay, blithe—immediately the sun

shines in our hearts. But to the stately tramp of the
mourners of Death the music steadies to more solemn and majestic cadence—at once the shadow of
Sorrow stalks in the land. A rollicking lilt from the
barrel-organ sets all the children's feet a-jigging
down the alley.

Reasoned Speech (written or spoken) is our *in-*
tellectual means of communion with our fellows.

Art is our *sensed* means of communion with our
fellows.

LET us be clear, here and now, not to confuse
Speech and Art. Speech as logical statement has
nothing to do with Art. It is only when words are
so compelled into such forms as we may call Make-
Believe by the artist in words—the poet in prose
or verse—that they arouse the poet's feelings in
us, that they become Art. Until *words* are so employed that they reach our intelligence through the
senses they cannot become Art.

Nor let there be any fumbling with the word
Emotion. By *emotion,* be it understood, is meant
everything that we sense or feel. There is danger
of tangle in using the word, since it has come to
be employed in a false meaning of extravagant

sensing. The word "emotion" runs the danger of being thought of as a mere agitation of the mind, or more often as emotionalism—a superficial or a violent excitation of the weaker or more uncontrollable sensings of the body. By Emotions are here meant the impressions, however varied, however deep or subtle or serene or overwhelming, however stupendous or peaceful or tender or delicate, upon the feelings, as separate from the Reason and the Thinking.

Unfortunately, again, the word *Impressionism* has come to a particular false usage in relation to the Arts; but Impression of the Emotion or Thing Felt is that which creates and is created by all Art whatsoever—emotion is its sole province, aim, and significance. No scientific theorising, no book-learning, no elaborate scholarship will enable us to perceive Art; no lack of such things will give us the power to perceive Art. The impression left upon our senses by a face, a character, by the moods of men or of nature—the impression left upon our feelings through our hearing or touch or vision or the like—all these are of the realm of the artist, and these alone. Art is that, and only that—but

all that. But, that confusion may be prevented, it
is well, instead of employing the words Emotion
or Feeling—which have certain restricted meanings
—to use the word "sense" as a verb as being the
basic essence of the act of Art.

It is the essential act of Art, then, by skill and
cunning of craftsmanship, to turn sensing into
such a form that it will convey to others the like
sensing that has been produced in the artist. That
is the essential quality of Art.

Art is in clear phrase a prodigious realm—the
Sensed Revelation of Life. Any act whatsoever
whereby a man communicates an impression into
our senses that he himself has felt is a work of Art.

If it be crudely done, it is crude Art; if finely
done, it is fine Art; that is the sole difference, but
the one is as much Art as the other.

ART is not an oil-painting on canvas in a gilt
frame. Art is not the exclusive toy of a few prigs—
nor the password of a cult. Art is universal, eternal
—not parochial. Every man is an artist in his degree—every man is moved by Art in his degree.
For one act of our day to which we are moved by

calculated Reason we are moved to a score by the
emotions, by instinct, by our senses—by the thing
felt.

Every child is an artist. When a child essays to
explain an experience, that child by instinct almost invariably utters that experience or sensation
in such terms as to make us *feel* what it has felt.
It at once becomes an artist thereby. A child is not
content to commune with us through its thoughts
—that is to say, merely by Reason, by speech logically employed; it endeavours so to turn words
about as to make us feel what it has felt—in plain
words, it employs Art. Art precedes Reason.

Simple people always endeavour, in rude fashion
enough, to interpret the effect upon them of things
felt. The simple folk employ Art even more than
they employ Speech. Their power to commune
with us through Art is prodigiously greater than
their power to employ Thought through Speech.
The very way in which we say Yes or No depends
for its result more upon the Art with which we
say it than upon the mere saying of it.

Around the camp fire rough men gather and tell
tales. They are artists—greater or less according to
their skill of craftsmanship. In camp or quarter, in

palace or cottage, in mansion or hovel, in church or
pothouse, joy bursts into song, or sorrow into refrain; the limner with wondrous hand's skill tells
what his eyes have seen, the singer utters what his
ears have heard, the hand moulds the clay into
shapes that are symbols of the emotions evoked by
forms, the painter catches the mood of the twilight
or the freshness of dawn, the actor by gesture and
voice shows how something sensed may be repeated
into the senses of others, whether it arouse laughter
or tears. They are all artists—in their degree of
skill as craftsmen.

ART, then, so far from being a mere dandified
luxury for the rich or for the entertainment of the
prigs, is an absolute hunger of every intelligent
being.

Art, so far from being a luxury of no utility and
of late development in man, was with him from the
beginning—has been with him always—and will
be with him for ever.

And insomuch as the arts of a people are base,
so will it reveal their baseness as a people.

Art, so far from being the little exclusive preciosity that the so-called artistic coteries pride them-

selves alone on understanding, is far removed from
that preciosity—and whilst these very coteries are
hugging themselves on possessing it, they are generally embracing a dead thing or a sham, the while
the very people whom they affect to despise are
partakers in the Reality.

If you would realise what your life would be
without the means to commune with your fellow-
men so as to be partakers in their sensations and
their emotions, try to think of a man in that awful
solitude that is never broken by contact with any
other human soul; and you cannot exaggerate what
a man's punishment would be without the Arts.
He who is without the Arts lives in a blind man's
parish; nay, worse, walks in the fantastic isolation
of the kingdom of the mad, little higher than the
beasts.

IMMEDIATELY we grasp the basic significance of
Art a vast and limitless realm at once opens before
the artist for his conquest and adventure. Whereas,
to-day, critics and artists bewail the fact that
"everything has been done," and that we can only
ring the changes on past achievement, Art is in
fact little more than beyond its beginnings. No

man may reach to the splendid wayfaring of life, or, indeed, know of life beyond an idiot's conception, without Art. It is the majestic road that every sane man must travel towards the immensities. The chief path by which man may reach to great goals and a larger experience of life is through the Arts. Whether by the oratory of a Christ, or by the drama of the masters, or by its many pathways, the road that reaches to the Splendid Wayfaring must be through the garden of the Arts. Whether he like it or not, whether he deny it or not, whether he realise it or not, every man must walk in the garden of the Arts. Some slink through it, others glory in the journeying; but walk it they must.

Chapter III

OF CRAFTSMANSHIP

NOW, just as Speech must be an *intelligent* utterance of Thought, so Art must be an *intelligent* utterance of Emotion—of the thing sensed.

It is not enough to have uttered a thought to account it Speech; otherwise we are but in a Babel of Strange Sounds, signifying Nothing.

Nor is it enough to have uttered emotion to account it Art. It is vital that the Emotion shall be so uttered as to arouse the like emotion in the beholder—otherwise are we in a tangled Whirl of Confusion.

Thus, just as Thought is the more perfectly-understood as it is deftly expressed; so is Emotion the more perfectly transmitted inasmuch as it is most perfectly uttered.

Art can only be created, therefore, by skill of handling, which is called Craftsmanship.

CRAFTSMANSHIP is the skill or cunning whereby we utter Art; whereby we create the body that holds the spirit of Art and gives it form and substance; Craftsmanship is the means whereby we give utterance to that which we have sensed, and hand on the emotion aroused so that others may sense it in like fashion.

In simple terms, by Craftsmanship we can create impressions by means of colours so that we hand on to others the sensations that have been aroused in our vision; or by employing words in such a form of prose or verse that these things become poetry so that we can convey into the intelligence of others through their sense of hearing not only our Thoughts but our Sensations, stirring in the hearing of others the feelings and impressions that we desire to convey. So with Music, or with other such like craftsmanship.

Supreme craftsmanship is the perfection of statement by and through which Art is uttered. By this Craftsmanship, by this cunning of skill wherewith the material—colour, words, sounds, marble, clay, bronze, or what not—is so wrought by the artist that by his wizardry it arouses in us the emotions, impressions, sensations, which the artist has left, he creates his impression, whether the sense of majesty, or of awe, or of pity, of suffering, of horror, of sadness, of joy, or the like.

Whatsoever the emotion, it can be created by the craftsmanship of the artist to whom has been granted the power and faculty, subtle, rhythmic, indefinable as life itself, to mould the wondrous thing so that we become partakers in his sensing. So instinctive is this faculty that artists can rarely explain it—they can only exercise it.

The moment that the artist, by his skill of craftsmanship, creates and transmits his impression to us, a work of Art is born.

ALL Art is one; but the crafts by which Art is uttered are many. Whether by sound or words or colour or what not, whether it be by music or oratory or painting or prose or verse, these are but the means whereby we utter Art; but to each craft is given power to utter Art in fitting fashion. The craft of painting gives forth emotions roused by things seen, through the sense of colour and form, which cannot be so fitly felt by any other sense such as hearing, therefore cannot be so fitly uttered by music. The craft of music utters emotions roused in the hearing, which cannot be so fitly evolved by any other craft, such as the craft of the sense of vision. So it comes about that each craft works intelligently only within its right domain; and any attempts to make one craft do what another craft could do better, must ever end in feeble artistry and bastard intention.

The hopeless misunderstanding of this basic fact has led philosophy and criticism into the morass of false dogma from time immemorial; so that we get such fatuous "laws," greedily swallowed, that music is the most perfect or pure or typical of the Arts. It is nothing of the kind. Every Art is the most perfect or pure or typical to him who understands the basic significance of Art; and is such in the degree of its perfection of utterance within the realm of the particular sense through which it utters itself, and which it alone can interpret.

The vast realm of the vision is the sole limitation of the art of painting, but it is its limitation; the wide realm of the hearing is the sole limitation of music—but it is its limitation. And so with all the Arts. Every impression that the eye can receive, every impression that can reach the intelligence through the vision, is a fit subject for the art of painting—but the moment another sense is invaded, the art of painting is debauched. So certainly as a painting requires a written description to assist its meaning, we may be sure that as a work of Art it is a bastard thing.

But fitness of craftsmanship to the Art it would utter is the only limitation to any craft or means of expression whatsoever. It can be judged by no law, or created by no laws but success or failure to create the impression within the perception of the sense through and in which it is aroused. As long as an impression through the vision is essayed by the painter, it matters nothing if you or I or the critic "like" or "dislike" the craftsmanship; the triumph or the failure of the artist lies wholly in the fact whether he has been able to transmit into our intelligence through the sense of vision the impression that he himself has felt. And it is significant that if the critic be "pleased" with an impression that the artist has tried to utter in the manner of another artist, dead or alive, which has no relation to Art and is a vulgar act of intellectual fraud, the critic hails it as a work of Art!

BUT—and mark this well!—Art is not Craftsmanship. A work may be a superb piece of Craftsmanship without being a work of Art at all. At no time in the history of man has there been greater need to mark the difference between Art and the Craft by which Art is produced than to-day, when most of our teachers, professors and critics, constantly bemuddle the one thing with the other.

Art must create. Art must transfer Sensation from the creator of it to us. Whatever the Craftsmanship, the act of Art is ever the same, one and indivisible—the communion of an impression upon the sensing of others.

Craftsmanship is that wondrous skill whereby we shape words or colour or sound or other illusive or rigid material into the rhythmic essense of that Make-Believe that brings Art to life; it has nothing to do with mimicry of old masters or other pedantry—it is that wizardry whereby the alchemy of the creator makes a fitting and appropriate body so that the illusion of the Make-Believe is set up for the giving forth of the impression that he desires to express—and it is that and nothing but that; but it is all that. You shall find it never by mimicry, whether of the old masters or of the new, whether of nature or of life! but solely by the power and the perfection by which the impression is suggested. Therefore the sole aim of Craftsmanship in Art is to interpret the impression fittingly.

And just as genius in the old masters painted pictures which raise the guffaw of the ignorant in being very often absolutely untrue to the mere realities and details of nature—and so far as they are untrue to such realities the guffaw is on the side of mere scientific truth—so also the genius of the modern masters does well to disregard the mere tricks and conventions of the old masters, and to create a means of impression wholly concerned with stating Art fitly and in harmony with the intelligence of the age, employed with fullest power to arouse the emotional impression, and rejecting all tradition whatsoever and all scientific accuracies of bald facts. He who is incompetent to utter an impression of life upon the instrument developed by his age, will not reach to the wider communion by harking back to mimicry of the tricks of thumb of any age, however distant; he stands confessed a Brain-Thief.

THE prodigious value of Art is that by and through it we are enabled to experience the life of others, both of our own age and of the dead generations. The artists of a past age uttered their age for all time; living artists can only utter their own age

—and all effort to utter any other age is futile. To attempt to utter their own age in the accents of dead men or others is Academism—and all Academism is death to Art. And yet the astounding fact remains that even artists often become content with the skill of craftsmanship with which they created one masterpiece—a skill that only fitted that one impression—and proceed, the rest of their career, to employ the same craftsmanship to create their further endeavour, thus becoming Self-academics! The monotony of even so great a master of painting as Velazquez brought him to a limited range of achievement as Artist, though it made him one of the supreme Painters of all time. And that which limited even the range of artistic utterance of Velazquez himself is blindly mimicked by painters who, weary of the mimicry of Michelangelo or others, cannot realise that any mimicry of any man is academism as debasing and withering as classical academism! They utter this falsehood of the Brain-Thief simply because they have no grip on the basic significance of Art. But as most of the academic and the critical shower their gushing and unstinted praise upon a masterpiece by Velazquez until they find it to be by some one else, when they forthwith considerably abate their ecstasies, the value of their praise is about as high as that of their dispraise. Every separate work of Art requires that the artist should create a craftsmanship best fitted to utter it; and the great artist never allows monotony of craftsmanship to benumb his intention—for the utmost skill of tricks of thumb will not create the work of Art, once it is unfitted to the statement of the emotion or impression desired.

The art of painting, perhaps more than any other Art, has suffered greatly from this limitation; no painter has conquered so vast an empire of the imagination as Shakespeare in the wide gamut of the emotions through words; the painter who has come nearest is Turner, whose range was prodigious.

THE quarrels that vex the Arts are almost always due to the bemuddling of Art with the Craftsmanship that is employed to create works of Art.

So, little academic souls, and such as preen themselves on being initiate in the mysteries of craftsmanship, gaze upwards at the false prophets of Art and cry: "Wonderful!" and "How true!" and

"He must be clever, for the common folk do not understand; therefore this must be a great man!"

For him who does not understand a work of Art, such work of Art does not exist—it cannot exist.

The quarrels of the schools are mere parochial warfare, concerned with tricks of thumb, with craftsmanship. The Isms—Impressionism, Realism, Idealism, Symbolism, and the rest of the jargon, concern the studios alone; are the chips in the craftsman's workshop. The artist may employ any Ism. That is his affair of selection of weapon. What he is compelled to do before he can create Art is so to employ his Ism or trick of thumb or what-not, that he shall create the Impression desired. Nothing else matters.

Chapter IV

OF BEAUTY

ART is not Beauty.

Nor has it aught to do with Beauty.

A poker may be a beautiful thing—it is not Art thereby. A photograph may be a beautiful thing—it is not, therefore, Art. A woman may be beautiful—she is not necessarily a work of Art.

But craftsmanship depends on perfection of statement by and through which Art is uttered; craftsmanship is, therefore, often, as a result of this sense of perfection, beautiful—but it is not the essential quality even of craftsmanship that it shall create a sense of Beauty, but that it shall convey Art with fittingness. For instance, craftsmanship must be rugged in suggestion in essaying to convey ruggedness of feeling; beautiful if essaying to convey Beauty; and the like.

To arouse the impression of concords, craftsmanship must employ concords; but it is impossible to express discord and tragic impressions by means of concords, since concord is a negation of those very moods. To utter discords and violences, craft must employ discords and violences if such impressions are to be created.

There are those who, parrot-wise, have repeated throughout the ages that Art is Beauty. There are far greater, far more profound, vaster, more majestic, more subtle, more dreadful emotions, more horrible moods, than are aroused by mere Beauty. The sense of Beauty is a noble and legitimate aim in Art; but it is not the only aim, since it is not the only impression in Life.

Art is as much concerned with tears and pathos and tragedy and ugliness and greyness and the agonies of life as with laughter and comedy and beauty. The dread of death, the detestation of treachery, the horror of fear, the awful sense of vengeance, the hatred of wrong, the promptings of terror, the lust to kill, the indignation at a lie, the agonies of suffering, the contempt of baseness and meanness, are all as legitimate a province of Art as the prettier emotions. All sensed activities are within the realm of the artist—the ignoble and the noble alike. Indeed, if we would make the ignoble to appear noble, by skill of suggesting beauty—and ignoble things are often beautiful enough—then we fail in artistry

—for Art may not lie and live. He who makes an unbeautiful thing appear beautiful commits the unforgivable lie; it is an essential act of Art to show the unbeautiful thing unbeautiful, the beautiful thing beautiful.

THE Greek genius set up Beauty as the ultimate goal of Life. It, therefore, set up Beauty as the ultimate goal of Art. Beauty being the aim of Life to the Greeks, they were justified in making Beauty the sole aim of their Art. The Greeks did really mean that Beauty of craftmanship alone was not enough—but that Art must create Beauty as its sole aim, "the Fair Thing."

But the world has moved to higher goals, to nobler aspirations, to a larger concept of life, than the Greeks knew or dreamed—and mere Beauty is no longer the ultimate aim of life, therefore no longer the ultimate aim of Art.

This falsity of making Beauty the end and all of Life, this absolute aim to achieve Beauty was the cause of the triumph of the Greeks in their Art—a greatly over-rated triumph when stated against the full significance of Life; a triumph of which the schoolmaster tells us much. It was also the cause of her limitations and of her eventual failure to achieve the complete and supreme mastery in Art —of which we hear little.

The Art of Greece achieved Beauty in wondrous fashion; but a mightier significance than Greece or Beauty reigns over life. Greece fell amongst the lesser breeds. Greece fell; and her Art fell with her, giving place to a vaster Art, a wider significance. In colour Greece never approached the artistry of the sumptuous Art of Italy, that gave place to the Art of Spain and Holland, which concerned themselves with the supreme significance of human character and of the varying moods of nature—a far deeper significance than mere Beauty holds.

IT was the aim of Classic Art to glorify Sameness —to create the Type—to polish man to an exquisitely perfect model in his outward seeming— to make the temples it reared and the homes it built a very Regularity. To the Greek the perfect outer man had two sides, the one the likeness of the other, as he stands upright and full-fronted to us, his right side the exact counterpart of his left. The Greek ideal ever chiselled to create the type, and made for the destruction of character—being a splendid an-

nulling of the *differences* that create character—
in order that there might be created the Unities,
smoothing away exactly those *differences* which
give the essence of the Individual. But the Greek
forgot that man is not all in his outward seeming
—that he has a heart within—that the within of
man is not as the Without, and the one side not as
the other.

IT was to them of the Gothic blood, to the peoples whose whole Art and glory are deep-rooted in
character—who give the bays of their homage to
character above all other human qualities, however rugged the body wherein that character flames
—it was to them who founded their genius on the
individual as against the classic ideal that seeks
Beauty alone through perfection of exact balance
—it was to the North (and, by some strange whim
of fate, to Spain, perhaps from her admixture of
Gothic blood of the North, her vision so akin to
the vision of the North) that Art revealed itself in
deeper fashion than in the mere outward seeming
of cold perfection. The rude, rugged North! It was
in the North, and Spain with the North, that por-
traiture came to its supreme achievement; that

character in drama found its most exquisite statement. For, always in the Life and Art of the North
you shall see this basic adoration of character—the
tribute to the difference of individuals. Watch how
the old monks pondered upon character, from their
illuminations to their majestic cathedrals, from
their saints to their devils—always the grim
feeling for character. Indeed, you will find the
eventual break-down of the mediæval Church in
that she forgot her wide-embracing arms of Cathol-
icism and became subject to the classic spell of
Rome, putting on a classic tyranny that sought to
grind down individuals to a type, thereby alienat-
ing the peoples whose very breath and being are
founded on the Liberty of the Individual. Their art,
their religion, their whole state are founded upon
character; grow in it; have blossomed upon it. And
it was only when the mediæval Church awoke and
adapted itself to the larger intention of life that it
saved itself from the destruction that threatened
its very foundations.

WATCH the exquisite agonies of the pencil of the
North! See how the eager eye of the North guides
the brush—searching out each little *difference* of

each *different* feature in everything upon which it
looks, where the Classic eye was wont to seek to
bring things to formal balance, and the Classic
chisel to carve down all irregularities to the type.
With what fastidious care the brush sweeps in
forthright mastery over the canvas, hand and eye
following each form that pronounces Character—
whether of a Dutch bottle, an apple, the cattle in
the fields, the mood of the hour, a devil on a cathedral gargoyle, a saint, or the distinction of man!

To them of the Northern blood, in all its many
diffusions, setting Character upon the altars of its
living faith, there was revealed (to the English and
Netherlanders and the French) a still deeper sense
of the mysteries, so that they have filched the
haunting sweet-sadness out of the twilight, the
mood out of the sunset, the ecstacies out of the sunlight's flicker among the leaves of the trees, and
the significance from the shadows. They have
caught the thunder and the roar, the peace and the
varying moods of the seas, with a subtlety and a
power and an inquisitive searching into the impressions of nature such as the ancient world scarce
dreamed of. They have sought in the labour of the
workers of the fields, and the swarthy toilers of

the market and the street and the factory, a lyric
theme for glory in the mighty industry of man;
and, in the tragedies and comedies that assail men
and women, have essayed to interpret the atmosphere and moods aroused by their stupendous endeavour.

Yet because the Greeks reached to a sublime
achievement in Art, the pedant and the prig, the
professor and philosopher and the critic continue
to lay down the Greek law that Art is Beauty!

To-day living Art concerns itself, and must concern itself, with the emotions that move humanity,
as Art has ever been concerned with the sensing of
life. And the mystery of it all is no less profound
than the searchings of the heart and the hunger of
the soul to know of life that moved the old Egyp-
tians to their fantastic and wide endeavour. Splendid as was the mighty achievement of Greece, she
never reached to the majesty and the grandeur of
that masterpiece of sculpture that stands upon the
edge of Africa, head and shoulders above her highest achievement, in the wondrous thing that men
call the Sphinx—a work of Art that moves the
homage of the world and of the ages. The genius
of Egypt spent itself upon the mystery of life—

and it moved thereby to the higher purpose and vaster significance.

FOR, when all's said, and the last eager craving desired, it is all a mystery, this wondrous wayfaring that we call Life. And it is well so, lest the reason reel.

That which is set down in clear explicit fashion; that of which the knowledge and experience are completely exhausted, shall not satisfy the hunger of the imagination—for the imagination leaps beyond it. That which is completely stated, stands out clear and precise; we know the whole tale; it is finished. But that which stands amidst the shadows, with one foot withdrawn—that which is half hid in the mysteries of the unknown—holds the imagination and compels it.

If man once peeped within the half-open door and saw his God, where He sits in His Majesty, though the vision blinded him, his imagination would create a greater.

Chapter V

OF THE MIGHTY ACREAGE OF THE GARDEN OF THE ARTS, AND OF THE VAST SIGNIFICANCES THAT DWELL THEREIN

ART concerns itself with tears and pathos and tragedy and ugliness and greyness and the agonies of life, as much as with laughter and comedy and beauty.

Neither Plato nor Whistler nor Pater nor Flaubert nor This One nor That One nor Another, has the right to narrow the acreage of the garden of life. What concern had Shakespeare with Beauty? What concern the English translators of the Bible? How far did Beauty guide the pen of Carlyle's superb prose? Or how much was Chaucer's aim kept upon Beauty? Who can point to Beauty as Hogarth's prime resolve in flogging the vices of his age? or say that Hals found therein the main endeavour of his genius? In the book that Shakespeare wrote, Beauty is not his god, nor Beauty his ultimate aim. Is jealousy beautiful? Yet "Othello"

is great art. Is man's ineffectual struggle against
destiny beautiful? Yet "Hamlet" is rightly accounted the masterpiece of the ages. Are Hate and
Despair and Fear beautiful? He who would show
these things beautiful would, in the very doing,
prove himself no artist, but a vulgar liar.

It has been solemnly written, by one dictating
public taste, that Millet's "Killing a Hog" is beautiful! It is wholly unbeautiful. Had Millet made it
beautiful, he had uttered the stupidest of lies.
Nevertheless, the statement of it is Art. Indeed,
Millet's aim in Art, a large part of his significance
in Art, is a protest against the prettiness of mere
beauty. He took the earth, this great-soul'd man,
and he wrought with a master's statement the
pathos and the tragedy and the might and the
majesty of the earth and of them that toil upon the
earth. He uttered the weariness and the gloom as
well as the sense of thanksgiving. He uttered the
ugliness and the bending of the human body and
the sweat of man's brow in the conflict to win
bread from the earth; and he did it, not by making factories look like campanili, not by concealing
in false impressions, but by revealing the grandeur
of the reality and significance of things by suggest-

ing the mystery of their significance. "The Man with the Hoe" and "The Sower" are far more than beautiful—they hold the vast emotions aroused by the contemplation of man's mystic destiny to labour, and of man's acceptance of that destiny; they utter the ugliness and the ruggedness and the sombreness of it, the awful wonder of it, as loudly as they state the beauty of the earth and the fearful discipline of toil; and they most rightly utter those wondrous and haunting and profound things, so that they take equal rank, and thereby add to our experience of life through the master's power of interpretation and skill of craftsmanship, whereby he so solemnly uttered their significance and their truth.

Had Shakespeare made jealousy beautiful; had he not made it hideous; had he made treachery and the lust to murder beautiful instead of hideous, he had uttered an unforgivable lie.

IF you shall confuse Beauty with Art, then must you discard many of the world's mightiest masterpieces.

Yet you will find this falsity so deeply taken root in prejudice, that the prig not only insists

upon Art being Beauty, but he strives, and strains
his meagre wits, to show everything that he sus-
pects to be Art to be likewise a thing of beauty—
he will distort and steep in casuistry the most hideous and tragic and horrible and ugly things, squeezing them into a strait waistcoat that he labels
Beauty, until he loses all sense of Beauty and of
the meaning of words in a quagmire of fantastic
babble. Nay, rather than reject masterpieces that
he cannot deny, he will swear away his soul that
they are beautiful, even though the fact of their
being beautiful would wholly damn their sublime
artistry and belie the intention of the impression
that the artist essayed to arouse! The phrase that
Art is Beauty has run so long that it has come to
be taken for a basic truth; and we get even men of
genius, in order to reconcile the unbeautiful with
the beautiful, reaffirming the stupid falsity because
some freak of "philosophy" or of "science" has
decided to vow Art to be a thing that "gives pleasure"—just for all the world like any prostitute
squeezing any damnable vileness into the corsets of
Beauty. They will even damn their own achievement, so that the words of their mouth murmur
the foolishness that the work of their hand's skill

must "give pleasure," or be "beautiful," or "amuse"!

William Morris defined Art as "the expression of pleasure in work." This might largely define the enthusiasm, indeed the joy, in achieving fine craftsmanship; but it has nothing to do with Art. It is not even a complete definition of craftsmanship; though to some extent, like Beauty, it is so, since perfection of handling, like perfection of anything, must generally produce an effect of beauty, or something akin to beauty. William Morris wrecked what might have been a great artistic career by essaying to employ the craftsmanship, and seeking to see through the spectacles, in prose and in design, of dead artists, whose age and vision were wholly alien to his own age and vision.

ART is the splendid garden of man's imagination, the wayfaring by which he reaches to the majestic realm of his fullest experience, the wide highway whereby he steps from his petty agonies into the vast communion of his fellows, inherits the ages, and reaches out to his fulfilment. Art is a garden wherein blossoms the richest and the largest knowledge of life, wherein man may find a harvest for

the reaping, abundance for the gathering. Without
Art he lives in the sordid garret of a paltry loneliness with his own petty soul. He has but to step
into the garden of Art in order to walk with the
giants; hold communion with the saints; know the
exquisite ecstasies of life; thrill with the impetus of
the noblest passions; enlarge his heart and brain
with the fellowship of such as have trod the vastnesses and have suffered with the broken, have
known pity and triumph, been purified by compas-
sion, and have strutted it to the stately measure of
heroic impulses. There is no sensation that he may
not experience, and, experiencing, live, if he shall
wander into the splendid wayfaring.

For, to such as walk in the garden of the Arts,
the eye may experience, the hearing thrill to, the
senses be excited by the sublime emotions that
others have felt and recorded with the wizardry
of the Arts through the wide immeasurable gamut
of the emotions—from the vastest and the most
dramatic to the subtlest moods and the most exquisite impressions. To such, the twilight will yield
its sweet-sad gloom, played into the senses by the
Art of a Watteau or a Corot, or uttered in song by
the skill of him who wrought the tense verse of

"An Elegy in a Country Churchyard." To such the Art of Shakespeare, by skilled magic of the weaving of words, yields the wide and sonorous sensations of a prodigious experience—an astounding range of emotions, from the exquisite pain of the love-lyric to the heroic impulse of war, and the large and majestic moods that make men near to the gods, whether they face the tragic sublimities or climb the firmament to highest ambitions.

SEATED before a book in narrow garret, lighted by flame of solitary candle, with the Art of such an one as Shakespeare made, 'tis given to us, yielding ourselves to the wizardry of his astounding skill in weaving words, thereby to experience emotions that the richest cannot more fully know. With the marvellous instinct that unlocked to him the music that is in words, he wrought the phrase's significances into impressions that move us in strange and compelling fashion. What science shall unknot the skill that makes the words take on their large and rounded forms? or moves us into the mood whereby we answer through our senses to the majestic utterance? At a trice the measure of the phrasing changes under the alchemy of his craftsmanship—he utters the rippling mood of laughter and sets merriment jiggling through our blood. A stately mood, and at once we are moving in more stately measure. The words drag in love-lorn ecstasy of man for maid, of maid for man, and we are held forthwith by the strange and haunting perplexities that the world calls Love. Again the measure of the words changes, and the agonies of life or tears or awesome dread take possession of us. Such things no laws can weave. The means escape us. We know that Art has been created, for we have become partakers in the revelation of life through the skill of another who has yielded into our experience a new sense that had otherwise been denied us.

And surely it is a splendid thing that we should have been granted through the Arts to walk this vast garden of life which we had wholly not known in our narrow parish, shut off from the communion of our fellows, our hearing and vision and senses only permitted to know the narrow alley of our own solitary pathway from the cot in the nursery to the death-bed.

Chapter VI

OF IMPRESSIONISM

ALL Art must create an impression upon the intelligence through the senses. Without impression is no Art.

There is a false creed of Impressionism grown up amongst us, whereby a few have filched, as excuse for their tricks of thumb, the title to a vast domain; so that your man in the street, your critic, and your babbler have come to speak of Impressionism as a fantastic and peculiar eccentricity that bewilders. Paint the rose blue, or the face green, the hair lilac, or the grass plum-colour, then they cry out that this is Impressionism!

But Truth is none the less Truth because Falsehood dogs its footsteps.

All Art is by its very essence Impressionism. Art is not concerned with scientific details of accuracy. Art is solely concerned with the impressions created by things upon the senses. If the artist can arouse in our senses an intelligent impression by painting a face green, he is wholly justified if he, by so doing, arouse the impression; he has no concern with the natural colours of the face except to arouse an impression that he has sincerely felt; nor will his merely painting a face in its natural colours of necessity create a work of Art. Art is not the map of a fact. The truth, as revealed through the Arts, is not the bald truth of facts, but the sensed truth of impressions.

On the other hand, by merely painting a face green in order to startle people into thinking him rather an "original" sort of person, a man is no nearer becoming an artist than if he did not paint at all.

Take a simple instance. If one shall have looked upon a carnival dance, the mere mapping of the details in colour or prose may give a photographic statement of the facts, yet need not be Art. But if colour or prose, employed with skill of craftsmanship, arouse in our senses the mood of revelry that has been stirred in the vision (or other senses) of the artist so that we become partakers in that mood, then, though all details of fact be absent, we get a work of Art. If by the employment of sombre colours we are made to feel a sombre mood; if by the employment of gay colours we are made to feel a gay mood, to the exact pitch that the creator of it would utter into our intelligence, then a work of Art is born.

Impressionism may be detailed, may be blurred, may be scientifically exact, may be scientifically wrong, may be utterly inaccurate as to facts of details; but if it create truth of sensation it is Art.

A lofty and imposing impression cannot be created by accuracy of detail—for the impression must inevitably be rendered petty by a petty survey of it. Therefore, the vaster and more compelling impressions, creating, as they must, resultant overwhelmingness of sensation, will ever leap beyond detail and assume majestic proportions. One cannot peer into the ornament of a hero's buttons and at the same time see his whole splendour. One cannot see the petals of a daisy and at the same time see the whole meadow, far less the glamour that the sun is spreading over the country-side.

There is therefore no artistic essence in detail itself or in lack of detail. Craftsmanship, if it would create Art, shall be made to attune its handiwork to the impression that it would create. By the power whereby it creates the impression desired shall the greatness of Art alone be judged. Not by law or lack of law, but by power alone.

IMPRESSIONISM is but another fuller word for the utterance of emotion—so that we become partakers in that emotion.

The artist, whether in colour or words or sounds, or bronze, must found his Art on truth; but the mere Mimicry of facts will not create Art, nor is it the artist's province. He is compelled to employ the objects of nature as the skeleton of his Art, since these are the symbols of life to him and his fellow-men. Were he not to do so, he could not reach the intelligence of his fellows—and it is of the basic significance of Art that it shall reach the intelligence of his fellow-men.

The artist has to take that which he desires to utter, and, by moulding it into a Make-Believe, to arouse an impression. But it is not enough that he shall say to himself, "This is an impression"; he must by such skill of craft create it that it shall arouse the same impression that he has desired to create in the senses of his fellows, so that it shall reach their intelligence as an experience.

Turner rarely painted direct from the scene before him; he made accurate sketches and notes, took them into his studio, brooded upon them, and then created a general impression from them. There is a saying of Turner's to a troubled brother artist, snorting the while at the mere "accuracy" in landscape that he called "map-making": "Don't you know you must paint your *impressions?*"

Chardin's phrase also uttered the whole law of Art, whether of painting or aught else, when he answered the boasting painter who was vaunting his discovery of the purifying and perfecting of colours: "What, sir!" cries Chardin, "you say that one paints with colours?" "With what, then?" asks the astonished other. "One *uses* colours," Chardin rebukes him in that deep saying, "but one *paints with the feelings.*"

"Painting," said Constable, "is another word for *feeling.*"

SO giant after giant has given forth the secret of his mastery in like phrase—always that simple truth that Art is the *impression of the thing felt*—a work of the imagination.

It is not enough for the painter to sit down be-

fore nature and paint a mere mimic copy of the
thing he sees. Such may achieve superb craftsmanship of the tools employed. It is not enough for the
poet in prose or verse to record in exact accurate
detail that which is before him. Such do not create
Art. It is the part of the painter, the poet of words,
the artist in whatsoever means employed, to arouse
in us the atmosphere and impression that the scene
has aroused in his senses, in order that he may
achieve Art. By no other means shall Art be born.

Photography is an astounding craft—a craft that
at times steps across the threshold of Art. It is often
a thing of rare and wondrous beauty. If Art for
Art's Sake means that Art is exquisite craftsmanship, then photography is a great Art. If Art be
beauty, then photography is a great Art.

One of the grimmest falsities set up by the professors concerning Art is the utterly debauched
sense that they have given to their beloved word
"æsthetics"; for the Greeks meant by æsthetic the
thing *felt*.

The wide confusion amongst the critics about
Impressionism had its beginnings in the French
studios after the war with Prussia. Monet and others,
coming under the revelation of Turner, saw that

mere Realism could not produce the most profound Art; so they essayed thenceforth to try and find the secret whereby Turner ranged so wide an empire of the moods aroused by landscape. They did not discover the whole revelation, but they did discover that colour could be employed like music, so as to arouse by its harmonies the moods of nature—in simple terms they found that Turner used colour like an orchestra. They saw that with the pale and tender harmonies of the dawn upon the waters of the lagoons of Venice he created in our senses the impression of the dawn; that with the sombre colours of the dusk or the dying sunset he aroused the mood of dusk or the dying sunset. And they took this mighty revelation to France. The critics called this broken-colour orchestration by the name of "impressionism," and sought for its significance in its craftsmanship—as they always do. They missed the full significance in the, to them, new tricks of thumb (as they always do); and to the tricks of thumb they transferred the title of impressionism! and to this day many of the critical faculty mean (when they mean anything at all) by impressionism the use of little broken flecks of colour wherewith to build up a design!

And, so fatuous is their logic that they now invent a new word, Post-Impressionism, to describe a reaction from Impressionism, whereby certain painters have gone back to mimicry of the arts and vision of savage man! As if impressionism were a slab of Time; as if one could have a Post-cabbage or a Post-jackass! This primal-academism—for it is as abject academism to ape savage man as to ape Michelangelo or another—has no relation to Impressionism whatsoever, and is a negation of it. Surely nothing could better prove the utter bewilderment of criticism to understand the very essence of Impressionism than this bastard and fatuous phrase Post-Impressionism!

ONE of the constant seeming paradoxes in Art is that the artist is such by instinct, not by reason. It would appear strange were it not that Art is based in the communion of men's intelligence through the senses, not through the reason. The artist creates by intuition, by desire to create impressions. But when he comes to try and explain why he creates, he steps down from "sensed" intelligence into the arena of the reasoned intelligence, and so employs a means of communion which has

no relation to his province. When he reasons or
writes about the Art that he practises and creates,
he generally contradicts or even denies all that his
instinct creates—not from any desire to deny it,
but because he has now stepped from the intention
of his career into the philosophic quagmire of the
critics' æsthetics, which at heart he only knows by
hearsay. He thus further confuses the truth about
Art by the very splendour of his high achievement
in Art! The greatest of artists may be a giant in the
utterance of the senses—he may be, and often is,
near to an idiot in his reasoning, often wholly contemptible in mere "intellect." By consequence, the
moment that an artist steps outside the realm of
Art to explain it in terms of reason, he almost at
once tries to reconcile his Art with what scientific
men have said about Art—and is lost. No men
wrote more consummate drivel about Art than did
Michelangelo and Reynolds and Whistler. And the
drivel being consummately stated, so much the more
deadly the evil. Whistler in particular wrote falsities
about Art, not knowing logically in the least what
was the function of Art; but, the reason being
laid aside and the brush in his hand, becoming under
the compulsion of high artistic instinct a superb

artist, he achieved such exquisite masterpieces that, by the very mastery of his artistic achievement, his fatuous reasoning about Art took on a vile authority—an authority all the more vile since he uttered it with a beauty and phrasing that was as fascinating as it was utterly false. The moment that he turned to the intention of his instinct Whistler shed all the falsities of his mouth from him; he gave himself wholly to uttering the impressions that had been aroused in his soul, and he stepped thereby amongst the immortals. His own Art done, turning to the Art of others, he revealed at once the narrow vision of his egoism; and was unable to see that in the very realm of which he was so distinguished a master he had not the range to wing into the vastnesses of such as were far mightier than he—he did not perceive, and therefore essayed to belittle, the genius of Turner, from whose stupendous shadow he peeped out but a pigmy.

But, you may say, if the critic and the professor of æsthetics do not know, surely the artists must know what is great Art! It does not follow. The artist may or may not have wide perception for the Art of others. But he who would range the realm of the masters must first rid himself of all æsthetic

laws, and discover the basic significance of Art—
the simple truth that Art is the "sensed" communion of our fellows. In the measure of his power
to receive the communion of the impressions of
the artists, and in that alone, shall he find fulfilment
of their Art. No books, no explanations of other
men can help him one jot or tittle—these can only
make of him an intellectual snob. The uttered impression reaches him or it does not. All else is futile.

WHAT fatuous drivel, then, to speak of Art being
Beauty! Art is not a parish, nor a toy. The whole
vast gamut of the emotions of mankind lie within
the prodigious realm of the artist for his charting.
The field of impression is illimitable as life itself.

Indeed, the professor and the philosopher, having
decided that Art must be Beauty, proceed to compel Ugliness and every sensation that is the very
negation of beauty into their falsity. But Beauty
and Ugliness are as the poles apart—they are the
extremes, the denial each of the other. It seems
almost fantastic that so obvious a truth needs to be
asserted. Yet they are as rightfully the realm of
the artist, the one as the other. Nay, more—the
moment that the artist seeks to make the one the

other, he utters the unforgivable lie. The moment that he would palliate the ugly and would essay to show it beautiful, he lies—and that most damnably. Perhaps the most hideous and awful thing that man ever did was to wound and gash and torture and crucify the gentle Christ; and the artist who puts forth his hand to show this hideous thing as anything but hideous and horrible—far more, as he so often did in the much-vaunted Art of the Renaissance, he who essays to make it appear beautiful—fails as an artist in the measure of his intention and achievement.

It is not he who shows vice to be vicious who sins against Art. Yet it is ever they who weave a glamour over evil things who cast shocked eyes to heaven when evil is shown to be hideous!

Chapter VII

OF THE INTELLECT AND THE SENSES IN ART

ONE of the most fertile sources of error as to what *constitutes* Art is created by the jumping of the critics and philosophers and the professors from standard to standard—now of Beauty, now of Intellect, now of Enjoyment, now of Pleasure, now of Love, now of Morality, and the like. None of these things is the basis of Art. They are all drawn into it; hence the confusion. But Art is wholly independent of them all. A work of Art may be a prodigious masterpiece and contain none of these things. The "Betrayal of the Christ by Judas" may rouse in our senses a prodigious impression; and, being uttered with power, may produce a masterpiece—yet were most of these qualities, claimed as essential to Art, contained in it, it would be a lie in Art! Masterpiece after masterpiece has been created that contains none of these qualities—and most rightly contains none, or had perished as Art.

The Intellect in particular has caused much fear-

fulness and searching of soul, as regards its relation
to Art. *We must beware of confusing Intelligence
and Intellect.* Let us define what we mean by Intellect. The man in the street roughly means that
part of the intelligence or understanding which is
concerned with Reason; and we can do worse than
to accept that rough description—the thinking machinery.

The direct communion of brain with brain, so
that one intelligence utters a Thought to another
intelligence, leaves the intelligence cold. Intellect
can say to intellect that two and two make four.
That is an intelligent statement of pure Reason.
Yet it is a fantastic fact that Reason, which prides
itself on pure Truth, has by deduction come to
such fantastic conclusions as that there is no time,
no space, and no matter—that these things are but
an illusion. But if a philosopher trip over his spectacles and fall off a cliff a thousand feet on to the
rocks below, he swiftly discovers that time and
space and matter are no illusion—and even as he
falls he will suspect that his Reason does not further
matter, though his brains be scattered matter.

Pure Reason has created a vast emprise for man
—it has brought forth science and mathematics

and mechanics and machinery and philosophy amongst other prodigious achievements to the increase of his splendour. Yet these had left his intelligence cold but for a far vaster communion —that means whereby he is moved to sublime endeavour and to his supreme achievements—the means whereby has been granted to him the communion of his sensing. And every means by which he so communes with his fellows is an Art.

The Intellect has nothing to do with the foundations of Art; it is not the basis of Art—if by Intellect we mean the seat of the Reason, the logical side of the intelligence.

Art reaches the Intelligence, or understanding, solely through the senses. Reason reaches the Intelligence outside the channel of the senses—is indeed suspicious of the senses.

A statement of pure Reason—the Truth as a statement of fact, of pure Reason—may be found in Art, and often is; but to reach the intelligence as a *perceived* truth *it must first be turned into terms of the senses.* Before a logical truth can be wrought into the fabric of Art, it must be taken and remoulded and compelled into imagery, into a Make-believe, since thereby alone is it able to enter into

our senses; that thereby it shall reach our understanding as the thing felt, not merely thought.

If, on the stage, an actor say, "I love this
woman," in a cold, reasoned statement, no Art is
produced. It is absolutely necessary that the actor
or actress shall so act that we have created in our
senses the impression that the man loves the woman.

It may seem at first blush to the loose-thinking
that, since Literature is the greatest of all the Arts,
Speech is as much the instrument of our Sensing as
of our Thought. But it is only when speech is employed in such a way that it disregards mere Reason and is compelled into such forms as to create
impressions through illusion and so arouse our sensing of these impressions regardless of pure Reason
that speech, like any other material, becomes Art
—becomes what we call the Poetry of prose or
verse. Indeed, it is precisely this subtle difference
between words used as a cold logical statement and
words used as material for the Make-believe, wherewith to arouse our sensing, that has caused so much
of the confusion as to the basic significance of Art
amongst the philosophers, the critics, the professors, the antique-dealers and the pedants.

A PLAY may be written that contains the most absolute truths of Reason; it may be written with great beauty; but it may be without a shred of Art for all that. It is only when those truths are compelled by the alchemy of Art into such forms, such a Make-believe, that we are made to feel them as sensations of life, that they become Art. An intellectual statement, Reason, appeals to the brain in its thinking capacity; Reason appeals to the head. A work of Art must grip the heart—catch at the throat—rouse us in the realm of our emotions; and then, and only then, can it reach the intelligence as a Reality. Only when Art has crept into our being through our senses, can it continue its journey to the intelligence.

This is not to say that the Senses and the Intellect are in conflict. They are not. They act together and support each other. It only affirms that, before an intellectual statement can appeal to us as an experienced truth, it must be wrought into such a form of illusion that we *feel* it. For instance, the Reason can say that it is a cold day; but Art can make us *feel* that it is cold.

A harsh suspicion of the senses has always made

the Puritanical and the so-called Moralist shy and
fearful of the Arts; but this fearfulness is due to
bigotry and ignorance, arising from the incapacity
to see that man's noblest attributes are due to the
nobility of his feelings, not to his mere Reason.
Thinking can think as basely as the lowest of the
senses and the vilest of the passions can reach. The
senses and the passions can range a vast and noble
realm that the noblest thoughts cannot outrange.
And it is only when the noblest thoughts can be
changed and compelled into experience that they
have their highest value. Thoughts that cannot be
transmuted into feeling are but barren splendour.

IT is just this magical quality that is the very essence of Art, that the artist can take rigid stone or
molten metal, mere pigments or black ink, a piece
of catgut stretched on a resounding surface, or
words or the like strange material, and with them
can so conjure that these things may be made to
arouse an impression in our senses so that we live
the experience designed by the artist.

And it is a part of the fantastic essence of all
Art that whilst it must, by consequence, utter the
realities, must be true, it has always to employ, as

means to create that truth, a Make-believe—a sham
—the painted surface, or the sculptured object,
or the actors, painted and arrayed for their several
parts, none of which are the things they pretend
to be, and it is essential that they should not be.

Before the artist can transmit the impression
that he has felt in his intelligence, he must set up
this Make-believe, and only when he has created
this Make-believe can he impel the impression on-
wards into the channel of the senses of his fellows,
to reach their intelligence.

Whereas a reasoned communion of thought is
transmitted direct from brain to brain.

AND this wondrous Make-believe whereby the artist fulfils Art—whereby the flame is enabled to
burn more brightly in the lamp—it may not be
brought to fulfilment by Mimicry of dead things.
The artist has to fan into flame a torch which shall
lead to further heights, and the outworn lamps,
that lie cast aside along the path that his adventure
has already trod, shall not avail him for his forward
illumination.

It is by his insight and deep vision that the artist
creates this wizardry. The means he employs are

myriad manifold; the rare craftsmanship is his affair alone. It is folly to say this man achieved magnificence by this means, therefore by this means
must magnificence ever be achieved. These tricks
of thumb are a part of the chips of the workshop.
They have their interest for the artist as craftsman. Yet they are at best but Isms, that find far
too great importance in all critical consideration
of the Arts. The artist is free to use every Ism and
all Isms, so that he but create Art.

The artist's significance is that he shall create
Art, not that he shall satisfy the critic as to what
the critic considers he ought to create.

THE realm of Art is ever being invaded by the
Reason, and its purity usurped thereby. One of
the most dogged forms of this falsity is Symbolism. The moment that a literary intention usurps
painting or the like, you shall find Reason to be
the prostitute and thief of honour. A symbol is
quite sound in Art, say in painting or literature,
so long as it is a vital suggestion that all can understand without explanations. For instance, Mother-
hood. But the moment that a painter sets up a
figure in painting which requires explanation, it

betrays the usurpation of Reason and is bastard
Art. The moment that an artistic statement is
baulked in its direct appeal to the feelings, a hin-
drance is intervened that slays impression. The pea-
cock, to the early Christians, meant immortality
—its use was outside the realm of Art and belonged
to the Reason. To-day it conveys no such intention. The symbol is rarely an artistic element; and
is generally a degradation of Art. By symbol being meant, of course, the arbitrary setting up of
a formal figure to represent something else, generally an attribute, such as, whimsically enough,
has long been considered the very essence of "im-
aginative" Art, and has been the curse of painting
in particular. Symbol in its wider and more vague
term, the concentration of an impression in a dramatic essence, is another affair, and artistic in its
utterance; but all Art may be distorted into such
a term, which is thereby valueless as a definition.
All vital Art reveals its own meaning. It is not the
province of Art to mystify or conceal, but to reveal—to increase the concept of life.

NOW it will at once be seen that theoretic reasoned thought (or philosophy), and the practical

application of reasoned calculation, which we call Science, are one channel of communion between the intelligence of man and man whereby he becomes partaker of the thinking of his fellows; whilst the Arts are the other channel of communion between the intelligence of man and man whereby he becomes partaker of the other's sensing.

The utter lack of philosophy and of criticism to grasp these basic facts of life has been responsible for vast confusion. It is responsible for the obstinately held falsity, the fatuous but plausible pseudo-philosophic chatter, given forth with such pompous solemnity, that Art is a Luxury, that Utility precedes and always preceded Art in the life of a people; responsible for the falsity that Art is the attribute of a people in decay—their swan-song. It is above all responsible for the eternal balderdash about this being an Age of Science, therefore an age inimical to Art—as though in some way Science and Art were destructive to each other! All great periods of artistic utterance have been marked by a prodigious activity in Science. The so-called Italian Renaissance was prolific in scientific discovery. The supreme period of British Art under Turner was a prodigious age of Science. It has always been; it always will be. The two channels whereby men alone rise to fuller fulfilment of life through communion of their intelligence, must always develop in parallel magnitude. Leonardo da Vinci was as great a scientist as artist; and in the same individual the two faculties may burst into flame. There is no conflict between Art and Science, for they never touch, and can never antagonise or destroy each other. And so far from Art being the swan-note of a people's might, let a people see to its artistic utterance before all else; let men beware of the day that Art is departing from them, for the hour of their humiliation is at hand—it is the knell of that awful silence that has come into their destiny which must fall upon all outworn endeavour—for vitality is departing from them, and they are about to pass amongst the lesser breeds, and to be thrust into the waste places of the earth that a more virile breed may fulfil the splendour of a fuller life for which they are unfitted by lack of sensing. The day that a people have ceased to realise that the increase of their brotherhood by and through the vastness of their sensing is at an end, no mightiest armaments, no

untold wealth, will save them from passing
amongst the lesser breeds. Nay, the very fact of
their richness in armaments and wealth will make
them the surer quarry for the plucking.

ART and Science are in no way helpful or inimical
to each other in their basic intention. Art never
ceases—will never cease, so long as human life endures. It will fulfil itself to highest achievement
when a people is at its fulness of splendour. But
Art will always be—as it has always been, from
Man's beginnings. Man cannot be without it, except as a beast, on all fours, eating grass or crack-
ing nuts. This has but to be grasped to discover the
cant that primitive man was more "artistic" than
civilised man.

And just as there can be no antagonism of Science and Art, any more than there can be antagonism of gooseberries and red-herrings, so there
can be no decay of Art until a people decay. But
when a people, repelled by the virile endeavour to
move towards a mightier achievement in the destiny of man, begin to look back to their beginnings as to a mightier age, so also will their Arts

recoil from forward fulfilment and their artists
fall to toying with mimicry of childish utterance.

For, whilst the utterance of a child is of enormous significance as the revelation of childhood, it
becomes in the mouth of the adult the chatter of
an idiot.

Yet we are assailed to-day by this preposterous
ordering—laid down with the aggressive self-
sufficiency of critics who would of their insolence
fling contempt on all who gainsay them, brand-
ing such as unknowledgable dullards—that the
"new Art" is to be the mimicry of the utterance
of savage and alien breeds! Indeed, the theory is
lucrative for criticism, since the very critics have
sufficient skill to mimic savage utterance, and are
busy at the business, bringing forth bastard children to this adultery with the dead.

Chapter VIII

OF THE SPLENDOUR OF THE PASSIONS

REASON has done harm as well as good for life. By losing the relation of the Intellect to the Emotions; by placing Intellect above the Sensing; by mistaking Intellect for Intelligence, the world has come near to looking upon the strangling of life as a splendid discipline—the which precisely it is not.

And since we naturally come to try and express our survey of life in terms of Reason, we as naturally are prone to judge life as an affair of Reason; thus we soon slip into neglecting any significance that Life has in itself except when its acts can be squared with Reason. And the next downward step into the falsities is to look with suspicion on the emotions, since they are largely indifferent to Reason.

Art having for its wide activity the realm of the emotions, reaches to its highest flights in the sublime element where emotion reaches to Passion.

All things used to excess, all great qualities debauched by extravagance, can become most deadly forms of evil. But the gulf between Licence and Liberty is as wide as the gulf between Liberty and Lack of Liberty.

Human nature is by instinct noble—its instincts are ever towards the heights. If you shall make a man subject to others, by the odd whimsy of our destiny you make a weak vessel. If you give him Freedom to develop his full faculties, you make him one of the Masterfolk. Ring the human round about with denials, and you create the Abject, the Hypocrite, the Base-of-Will. Give the human his Liberty, and he soon realises that he cannot be free amongst the Masterfolk except by and through splendid self-discipline. If you shall grant a man freedom and he abuse it, setting up as his freedom alienation from the high companionship of the Masterfolk, be certain that he is born of the Slavefolk—it is not the Freedom whereby he falls, but in that he is unable to live free; he cannot live except by bond. He mistakes his petty parish for the world. He takes his enmity of the little, his tyranny over the groundlings, and his contempt of his fellows to be more virile than the companionship of the great. He looks upon splashing in a puddle as finer seamanship than sailing the ocean.

Of a truth, if you be dullard enough to accept the grey blasphemy that, at base, man is born a liar and a scoundrel and a miserable Sinner and that the truth is not in him, then it were well ever to obey the law Thou Shalt Not. But man happens to be born with eyes for the stars, feet to climb to the heights. His passions and his emotions and his instincts guide him to honour himself, to respect himself, to abhor tyranny, to hate cruelty, to be angered by injustice, to scale healthy ways and know virile habits. His very conceit impels him to the romantic ideal of himself. The Giver of Life made man to enjoy and exercise his functions, or wherefore gave He them to us? Man was not born for a monk's cell, nor woman for a nunnery—or we perish.

The small-eyed and the fearful speak ever of the great emotions which become the Passions, as being the evil side of us. Whereas, as a matter of the first importance to us in Life, our Passions are the best in us. It is the noble Passions that lead us forward, that impel us to life; and he is a born criminal whose baser passions overwhelm his nobler passions.

Make no mistake about it: all the moral codes,
all the dry philosophic jargon of Reason, all the
appeals to law, are as nothing in a man's life set
beside the high incentive of his passions—set beside
the impulse of his emotions increased to such tense-
ness that they become passion—for it is the strife
of his nobler passions in conflict with his lower desires that creates his conscience; which, indeed,
spurring him to action, creates the wider experience
of his soul.

There has been no great advance in the life of
man except that which has been wrought by the
noble passions—acts done in the thrill of heroic
fever born of the heroic impulse.

The intellect is the guide to knowledge of facts;
and the affairs of the intellect are mighty affairs
for the welfare and advance of man, but the intellect is sterile unless wedded to the emotions.

In religious observances it is not in the mere
laws and the moralities in his creeds, or in the
words of his mouth of a Sunday, but in the acts
of his will and conduct during the week that man's
nobility dwells. Formal things have their uses—
and often splendid uses. But it is not by prayers
or lack of prayers, by confessions or lack of con-

fessions, by symbols or lack of symbols, by idols
or lack of idols, by priests or by lack of priests,
that the Splendid Wayfaring of Life may be trod-
den; all these may help; but it is through the noble
intention made manifest by noble acts alone—by
the emotions and that which the emotions create.
It is not by his Thou Shalt Nots, but by his Thou
Shalts, that man reaches to the heights, walks to
fulfilment of the vast realm of life, knows Reality, and breathes nobility.

It is not by hiding behind vast fortifications that
worlds are won and conquests made.

SO, too, it is not by virtue of the observance of the
ritual of dead genius, but by the acts of creation
that genius and Art are brought to birth. The prig
and the pedant have so long misunderstood the
basic function of Art that they have set up petty
and pretty things as the narrow domain of Art,
and have hugged themselves in that they hold the
exclusive key to the little parish. But the province
of Art is vast as life itself. Whatsoever a man can
feel, whatsoever lies within his sensing, is the limitless acreage of the artist. The more vast his range
amongst the emotions, the greater the artist as

artist. And he is the mightiest artist, not like Velazquez, who is the most consummate craftsman in
a narrow realm of "sensing," but who, like Shakespeare or Turner, has winged the widest and highest flights through the emotions, and has uttered
them to his fellow-men. And surely it is a prodigious achievement to have made mankind feel pity
for what is pitiful, horror for what is horrible, joy
in what is joyous, tears for what is tearful; to have
wrought into the senses of his fellows the mood of
the dawn and the sunset, the storm and the impression of still waters; to have filled him with the
urge of ambition, the thrill of mighty endeavour,
the glory of the majesty of life!

The churches were once the sole guide to the
people in their forward moving; they employed Art
at every hand. The churches have largely ceased
so to be, since the Art of literature has brought
the communion of man into the narrowest home.
The newspaper took up for awhile the purification
and uplifting of the People towards a fuller life;
but the Press has largely passed into the commercial
intention, shackled by financial gain, and in the
measure of its corruption to such inartistic end has
it fallen from its artistic power, seeking wealth by

pander to the desire of the people rather than by
leadership to the fulfilment of life. So do, and will,
all the activities that employ Art, the revelation of
the fuller life to the people, on being debauched,
always pass from the purity of their artistic intention to a less virile purpose. But other activities become the lamp of Art; and it is to the novel and
the theatre that they who would know of life now
largely go—for it is the artist as always who en-
larges the garden of life.

THE appeal of the theatre is so direct, so vitalising,
that it is in the theatre more and more that the
artist essays to enlarge the garden of man's splendid wayfaring. A drama of the theatre is vastly
more compelling than the emotions aroused by any
other Art. Every day the inquisition of man into
the profound significances of life, and the revelation of the artist, trend more and more to utter
themselves in the theatre. To the artist must we
always look for the enlargement of the domain of
life. For the artist concerns himself with Life, and
only by Thou Shalt is Life created. It is in Art—
in letters and the drama, and its many other mani-
festations—that the creative instinct that adds to

the sensed life alone abides; and it is only through the Arts that man can come to a fuller concept of life than through his own solitary adventure.

ART is a majestic significance. And he who would mar it is the sourest of blasphemers.

But Art, like religion, can be debauched—and no Art has known viler debauchings than the Art of the theatre. The moment that an Art becomes the pander and the pimp to the traffickers of the market-place, it is lowered.

For the passions may be base as well as noble. The base passions can be as compelling and as powerful as the noble. The Art that creates ignoble passions may be as powerful and as fine in craftsmanship as the Art which creates the noblest passions. The artist is great in the measure of his power to create the emotions, whether noble or ignoble. But he who creates this ignoble intention is great in ignobility, and his truth the no less ignoble in that it is true.

Then, says your narrow of mind, we must set up a moral Censor who shall not permit ignoble Art. The which sounds moral enough in the saying. But it is for a people to have the will to pass

by ignoble Art; not to hand its will to any individual to tyrannise over. The Arts are ever threatened
by the debasing tyranny called Censorship far
more than they are threatened by the vilenesses
of base artists. Indeed, it is the experience of the
ages that a Censor will permit Vileness to parade
in Art if it be but arrayed in pleasant apparel, but
will always assail an Art that shows vileness to be
vile. No people are a free people who live under
the Censorship of the Arts by deputing another to
censor an Art, or who permit a tyranny. A Censor
is the deputation of a people's hypocrisy—has always been—will always be. For a people that have
not the mastery and self-discipline to survey all
Art, are tickled by the baser passions; and have
not the courage for the forward adventure amongst
the nobler passions—so that fearfulness becomes
their buckler. In their dread of facing the baser
impulses they tread a flowery path of mild emotions, too timid to walk the more dangerous journey of a rougher wayfaring; and thereby the wider
adventure is hidden from them. They weaken their
will and defence, and they lessen their range of
living. He who becomes partaker, through Art, of
the remorse that the sinner suffers is strengthened

in will as against him who dallies with the glamour
of vice but turns his sensitive soul from the despair and sordidness of him who travels the wayfaring of vice—his humiliation, and his shame. But,
worst of all, his soul becomes so narrowed that, not
only has he no heart for his weaker brethren, but,
from fear of his own weaknesses, he dreads a large
adventure and essays ever to compel upon mankind
as a virtue the timid wayfaring of a fearful and
timorous entity.

SO widespread is the desire of the fearful to compel their weakness upon their fellows as a virtue,
that to the mediocre the Passions have come to
mean the baser instincts and frenzies of man!
They forget that it needs a passionate love of his
fellows to send a man gladly to his death so that
another shall live—the which is accounted the sublime sacrifice. There is no great act of man that
thrills the imagination of the world that has not
been urged by a sublime emotion, where cold and
calculated Reason, had Reason been the sole incentive, would almost invariably have baulked the act.

Chapter IX

OF ART FOR ART'S SAKE

OF a surety Art is for Art's sake; as an Ass is for an Ass's sake. But when a man shall tell you that a door-scraper is for a door-scraper's sake, be you sure, and he sure, what you mean by door-scraping.

When a school arose, but awhile ago, that had for its battlecry "Art for Art's sake," it really meant that Art was for Craft's sake—that the goal of Art lay solely in the beauty of its Craftsmanship. It meant nothing else, pretended to mean nothing else, and arrogantly prided itself on meaning nothing else. These sneered at the "subject" of a work of Art as being of little or no importance. The handling of the craftsmanship was to be the sole aim in a work of Art—indeed, alone created it into a work of Art! This blasphemy to the splendour and significance of Art were as though one said that the Creator made the body of man as the supreme achievement—that man's character and soul, his emotions, his passions and his yearnings, were of little or no account. They would have the play of "Hamlet" without the Prince of Denmark. In the shallows of their confusion, in the deeps of their unthinking, what they said was this: that if a master-hand paint a wall white, by his mastery of trick of thumb he creates the poetic! that he thereby achieves a work of Art; that if an exquisite harmony of blues and greys and greens and such-like be set upon a piece of canvas with such skill as to please the eye and produce beauty, these thereby create a work of Art! That nothing else signifies but the exquisite handling of a medium!

This curse of the mere pursuit of Craftsmanship, in mistake for Art, has lain like a blight upon artistic endeavour up to this day, and has ever brought forth the decay of Art.

THIS false concept reached to its fullest danger and tyranny when Whistler, a superb artist, uttered it in the exquisite falsehood of his famous oration, the *Ten O'Clock*. Scarce a word of this was original thinking—he brought it from Paris; he clothed the phrases in polished and witty forms and uttered it as his own intention. But the Whistler who employed the Art of painting of which he

was a consummate master in his degree, was a far
different Whistler from the Whistler who employed
the Art of prose, of which he was only a superb
craftsman, not an artist. Whistler, by the words
of his mouth, would have us believe that it is the
province of Art to say Nothing very beautifully.
His instincts and his practice, his genius, made no
such mistake. No man's hand and brain ever gave
his mouth the lie in more frank and splendid insolence than did his. When Whistler stepped out
of his province, as an exquisite artist in colour, into
the realm of literature, he came into a kingdom in
which his sense of artistry in colour led him by
instinct to astounding craftsmanship of words—
he employed words as he employed colour; and in
the doing he proved how absolutely the methods
of the two Arts are one. But he failed in that his
instincts could not produce *Art* in letters, as surely
as they were unable to produce anything but Art
in painting. He gave to the world, clothed in beautiful raiment of words, modelled with consummate
craftsmanship, a book of Criticism of Art which
is as sorry a Falsity as was ever written by a great
artist on his Art—a book that, were it not a falsity,
would condemn his Art out of his own mouth—a

book that has destroyed and wrecked the poten-
tial power to create Art in more young painters
of his following than any one of the many fatuous works written by great artists aforetime has
wronged a great man's disciples and turned them
from the splendour of their master's ways. The
studios of painters are full of the ghouls of such as
have committed suicide in Art, dwarfed their powers, nay wholly blotted them out in the dread career of nullity—hanged by the neck to the silken
cord of Whistler's *Ten O'Clock;* for, legions of
damned careers listened to the words of Whistler's
mouth instead of reading the open book of his
great achievement; just as aforetime Barry lost his
soul in hearkening to the words of the mouth of
Sir Joshua Reynolds, essaying to create the masterpiece in the manner of the Great Dead whom Reynolds ever held up to the student, but which Sir
Joshua himself shrewdly avoided in the practice
of his own hands and the exercise of his own instincts.

WHISTLER was a master of emotional statement
in colour. He gave himself wholly to the right instinct which impels an artist to utter the revela-

tion of life in such terms as his skill of hand can
best essay. In the presence of Nature he took from
her the mood of the thing seen, the emotion it
aroused in his senses; and he set it down with so
fine and subtle a craftsmanship in colour that the
harmonies of his palette instil in us the same emotions—the rhythm of his colour is poured into our
vision in just such exquisite fashion as the magic
of music by a master pours into our hearing and
compels our imagination. The mere dross of the
paint and canvas falls from it; and there is revealed to us that which is above paint and canvas
—the mood of the thing seen, the impression
aroused in the senses, the hour of the day, the whole
subtle significance of it all, wrought into perfect
utterance by the skill of a magician. And this wondrous miracle of the hand's craft being so, we are
tempted in our blindness of intellect to seek for it
in the mere beauty of the mere clay of the body
that held it—and we are dullards enough to raise
the exquisite craftsmanship of the paint on the
canvas to the exalted state of the emotion that is
created through and by means of it. And, if we be
brazen enough to bray, we cry out that the Sensation is the Little—the clotted pigment, the flow-

ing oil, the warp and woof of the canvas, the
Great!

It is no mitigation of our humiliation to plead
that Whistler himself, when he was talking, should
have avowed falsities as his creed which his practice was incapable of committing. Nay, was it not
Whistler who gave us the most fatuous definition
of Art uttered by man's mouth? He said that Art
was *the Science of the Beautiful*—which were no
mean definition of Craft; and had been no bad
definition of Art but that Art is not a Science and
is not Beauty. It is of the wisdom of the wiseacre
who defined a Crab as a scarlet reptile that walks
backwards—which were not so bad, were it a reptile, were it scarlet, and did it walk backwards!

IT is not the least significant part of Whistler's
career that whilst in following his instinct for artistic utterance in painting he was incapable of
a falsity, in attempting to utter himself in literature he stepped out of the realm of pure impressionism into the realm of logic, and whilst he mastered and achieved complete and consummate skill
of craftsmanship in words he debauched the province of literary art by essaying to misuse its crafts-

manship to express ideas which were not born out
of the sincerity of his own intention in painting.
And so deep in falsity were the foundations of his
literary utterance that he could but build a structure of falsities upon them. And it is not the least
fantastic part of his defeat that the most precious
passage in his literary craftsmanship should contain
flagrant falsehoods, petty conceit, and mean understanding. Scan it for a moment:

"And when the evening mist clothes the river-
side with poetry, as with a veil, and the poor buildings lose themselves in the dim sky, and the tall
chimneys become campanili, and the warehouses
are palaces in the night, and the whole city hangs
in the heavens, and fairyland is before us—then
the wayfarer hastens home; the working man
and the cultured one, the wise man and the one of
pleasure, cease to understand, as they have ceased to
see; and Nature, who, for once, has sung in tune,
sings her exquisite song to the artist alone, her son
and her master—her son in that he loves her, her
master in that he knows her."

Here is a man priding himself on his "poetry,"
wholly unsuspecting that poetry, like all other
forms of Art, does not conceal but reveals—glory-

ing in things not looking like what they are but
like what they are not—as though a warehouse or
a Chimney should not have as noble a significance
as a palace or campanile!—unable to realise the real
romance, but seeking exultingly, the rather to put
a false idea upon a truth—and, not content with a
bridge or what not, not even content with a false
impression, but pouring his sour scorn upon others
in that they do not see falsely with him! Of a mind
so petty and a conceit so vast that he insolently ac-
cuses all but the professional artist of being unable
to see the exquisite beauty of the vision of nature;
incapable of realising that multitudes see it with
as deep and reverent, with as subtle and exquisite senses as he, though they may not have been
granted the wondrous gifts to utter the things
seen! So set on exalting the artist that he denies him
to be a wayfarer, a worker, cultured, wise, or
capable of pleasure! Indeed, it would be difficult to
count the swarming falsities, hiving like bees, in
that short passage; difficult to discover a single
phrase of unadulterated truth in it! difficult to
imagine a man in the presence of so exquisite a
vision only bent on disparaging his fellow-men!
The consummate tricks of craftsmanship of it

cover a raw sentimentality, mawkish as a seducer's
love-letters, vulgar as lard, contemptible and ill-
seen. But of true Art, not a tittle. For true Art
cannot lie.

Craftsmanship must be mastered, 'tis true, that
Art may be uttered; but the very mastery of
craftsmanship itself is a danger to Art, since the
keen desire to master it leads the artist only too
often to the pursuit of mere craftsmanship to the
utter loss of the aim of Art; which is as though a
fine lamp needed no flame. It is indeed possible for
a man to be a superb craftsman but no artist.

Half the fallacies about the Arts are due to the
confusion of this Make-believe with the Impression
that it is intended to create through that Make-
believe.

WHISTLER wrote of Art but to belittle it, as he
belittled his manhood and betrayed smallness of
soul in the pages of that paltry confession of his
pettiness that is the apology for his sour wayfaring
in the affected volume of his *Gentle Art of Making
Enemies*, wherein, essaying to bring his fellows into
contempt, he betrayed into what shallows he could
stoop his exquisite genius, even whilst he punished

his contemptible revilers and sapped the pretensions of the pompous. But think of a man glorying in publishing a whole volume to prove the cleverness of the paltriness of his own soul, that he might draw shrill laughter from the wry wits of the groundlings! with scarce a line to prove a large and generous vision or a genial mood of affection.

It was exactly in his confusion of Art with Beauty that Whistler fell short of the vastnesses. There are far greater, far more profound emotions than such as are aroused by mere beauty; and it was just in these very majestic qualities, in the sense of the sublime passions and of the immensities, before which his exquisite and subtle genius stood mute. It was his very narrowness of vision and limit of soul that made him pride himself on being unable to understand the eagle flight of Turner and to be bored by Shakespeare. But at least one of the greater senses was granted to him in abundance—the sense of the mystery of twilight. His instinct told him that suggestion was the soul of craftsmanship, and kept him from the blunder of mimicry. He never over-stated the details of life. Out of the mystic twilight he caught the haunting sense of its half-revelations and its elusiveness, and was given an exquisite emotional use of colour to utter these subtleties; and in the seeing he caught a glimpse of the hem of the garment of the Great Designer.

Chapter X

OF THE BRAIN-THIEF

THE living generation had its beginnings amidst a fierce strife of challenge to establish spiritual revelation. But to challenge ancient and established philosophy in its stronghold of tomfoolery of Æsthetics is even to-day as though one committed an intellectual blasphemy. Spiritual truth, so far from destruction, shedding the dross of centuries, emerges purified by fire. Sensed truth lies still under a very dunghill of decayed rubbish.

And the incubus upon all truth is ever Academism—intellectual snobbery.

Man's worst enemy to forward endeavour is intellectual snobbery. The young Napoleon was the selfsame Napoleon at nineteen as at death; but he had to beat down the tradition of the Napoleons of the Past before he was accepted; and, having beaten down the world, he was set upon the altar of men's intellectual snobbery, grew into fatuous proportions and bulk, and is now the pasteboard god of tyranny against further fulfilment. Rembrandt and Hals were scoffed at and rejected whilst they enlarged the conquest of the vision of man; and were buried in paupers' graves that the foolish words of the academic Brain-Thief might befool their age; the dullards grew fat in self-assurance, and were buried in filigree tombs amidst pomp and ceremonial; and now the Brain-Thief has set the rejected upon his altars and has made their high achievement a whip for the coming generations! How fantastic the human!

The Slave-mind is ever timid of testing its gods by fire; it shrinks from discovering to be tinsel what it is more comfortable to take for gold; the Masterfolk prove their gods before they set them upon the altars of their faith—for they are without fear and set comfort below forward-moving. The sword of the Masterfolk must have been tried by fire or will break in the splendid adventure towards the heights.

WE are come, then, to this: that Man has risen above the brutes and has reached to dominion over the world as the supreme lamp of Life and through his power to commune with the intelligence of his fellows, and thereby to increase his fulfilment and

their fulfilment by two roads to the intelligence—
by logic and by sensing—Reason and Art. We have
seen that Man must progress towards ever higher
heights or fall back amongst the lesser breeds. We
begin to realise the stupendous significance that is
Art—that the realm of Art is illimitable as Life,
eternal, has been from the beginning, must always
be as long as human life endures, since by it alone
man comes into the mighty heritage of this intelligence of his race or must remain little higher than
the brutes.

We now come to this: that Art, being the means
whereby, through a Make-believe, man communicates into the intelligence of his fellow-man the
impressions that have been aroused *in his sensing*—
realising that Art is only that, all that, yet nothing
but that—it follows that, vast as is his realm in
Art, by the very basic faculty of his achievement,
by the very essence of Art's significance and existence, *the artist has no power whatsoever to utter
anybody else's sensing*. The moment he essays to
filch the vision and utterance of another man
he is guilty of an inadequacy and, in uttering it,
a lie.

Now, this effort to mimic another man's vision is

Academism. The whole province of the Brain-
Thief is Academism. And all Academism is death
to Art.

'Tis true that when critics speak of Academism
they have at the back of their minds a vague idea
of a cold scholastic influence exerted on the Arts
by the artists of classic days—particularly the
Greeks. The vice of Academism is far more deadly,
far wider and deeper than mimicry of the icy regularity of the mimics of the Greeks.

Academism is the endeavour of a would-be
artist to filch the vision and employ the utterance
of another man. The Academic compels his powers
to mimic the craftsmanship of another man—mistaking thereby the significance of Art and of
craftsmanship—and, coming to skill in mimicry,
he mistakes this mimicry for the utterance of his
own personality and for Art! Even when he has an
impression, instead of essaying to utter it with his
own voice in a manner befitting that impression
and fitting nothing else, he looks about to see how
the great Dead or the great Living would have
handled a kindred theme; and he tries to utter it as
he thinks they would have uttered it. He has so
scant a concept of the basic intention of Art that

he borrows the spectacles of others; and he is under
the fantastic delusion that he can create a true impression of what another has felt! He does not see
that this is the very negation of Art.

The artist—whether painter, poet so-called,
sculptor, musician, or what not—creates by instinct: because he must. He may arise in the palace
or the hovel; but he is an artist in one sole achievement—a vast achievement—in that he is impelled
to communicate to his fellow-men the impressions
aroused in his senses by life. But the critic—he
who would codify in a system of laws the means
whereby the artist utters himself—proceeds to
judge all Art by the measure of the achievement of
the great dead masters; it is inevitable that he
should so blunder; he has no other means of setting
up his "science" and of drawing up his laws, but by
the standards of the achieved thing. He is, by consequence, out of date before he is born. Life has
passed on. But his theories catch the professors;
seem plausible to the man in the street; and thereby
his infertile endeavour becomes a tyranny. The
artist, inarticulate to describe or to account for
what he does, or why he does it, falls back under
servitude to the tyranny of the critical Reason,

which does not in fact guide him one tittle in his
own acts of creation, but which is a tyranny that
he either half-convinces himself he ought to accept,
or that he accepts in order to distort it to excuse his
own practice. This is the artist's first surrender.
Tyranny ever advances on a surrender. The next
surrender of the artist is the step towards the gates
of death—he proceeds to create an Art like some
one else, by preference an established dead master;
thereafter he is not interpreting Life as its impressions are felt through his own personality, but imitates instead the utterance of others, says what he
thinks other people would have said. Decay has
fallen upon his Art. He is become an academic.
Thereafter Art gathers her cloak about her and
sadly departs from him.

Now, do not let us for a moment shrug our
shoulders at this departure of Art from a people as
being but some superficial loss that does not much
matter—it means that vitality is departing from
the race, that its mastery in the world is gone.

TIME and time again history reveals, leads, and
warns; yet your solemn professor is deaf to it all!
Like a deep-voiced Litany the tragedy of the death

of Art is sung to him out of the ages, but he cannot hear; for his brain is bemuddled with a fantastic jumble of theories about Beauty or what not; and the simplicity of the truth is hidden from him even whilst he trips over it, his eyes bent instead upon a vast dunghill of rotting theories—the mess of futile things.

Nay; as though he shouted wisdom, he turns and denies that Art can be defined at all, even whilst he keeps defining it falsely; proving false, he shrinks at last from his own definitions, since he comes upon masterpieces that tear his definitions to shreds. Therefore, since *his* definition is false, all concept of Art must be impossible! As a simple fact, Art can be defined as far as Life can be defined; we can place its activity within the field of its significance, which is all the definition we need —but we do need to realise what is the true realm of Art. Definition is only a logical attempt to settle the significance of a thing, and has no other value, but has that value. It is futile, however, to lay down a definition that does not contain Art; and then, because masterpieces burst through that definition, or do not even come within it, to squeal shrilly that it is indefinable. Before we can survey

Art as an activity, the first need is to understand its basic significance, its achievement, and its consequence. We must understand what exactly is Art —and what is not.

The realm of Art is prodigious; next to Life itself the vastest realm of man's experience. It is universal, immeasurable, limitless—as life is universal, immeasurable, limitless. Its sole limitations are the limitations of life—and life is limitless. Individuals die, and individual Art dies; but life goes on and Art goes on. As long as there is conscious life, so long will there be, and must be, Art—for conscious life cannot be without Art, or would go mad. There is nought into which Life ranges that Art does not range, and has not the right to range— therefore, like Life, it is beyond the laws of criticism or criterion, cannot be created by Law, and is above Law. Its range is the whole wide flight of the Imagination; and it has the right, indeed it is its whole basic function, to utter the sensations of all life, from the loftiest heights of the passions to the lowest impulses in a dunghill. But—and here is the whole simplicity and awful truth overlooked by bookish men—one right it has not: it may not lie and live. One thing is denied to Art—it has no power not to be Art. The moment that Art attempts to lie, it is hideously or prettily a dead thing. Great Art can show the hideous to be hideous, the beautiful to be beautiful, the pleasant to be pleasant, the sorrowful to be sorrowful; but the moment it attempts to make an ugly thing appear to be beautiful it is a sorry lie, a sham, and an abomination. It dies, and it deserves to die.

NOW, one of the most deadly forms of lie in Art is the thieving of another man's utterance and the parading it as one's own. The moment that a man essays to utter other men's senses, he is a convicted thief in Art; and vital Art is not in him. He has become an academic. The whole realm of Art is gone from him, for it is the basic essential of Art that a man shall utter the sensed impressions of life as *he* has *felt* them.

Yet it is this very academism that is mistaken for Art by prigs and pedants; this very academism that is rewarded officially and by coteries; this very abomination that is by the very fact of its existence the standard and measure, the realm, and the pursuit of most Criticism. For there is no limit nor law in Art, there is only vital instinct to create it;

whereas Criticism almost inevitably founds on law; and the law of dead Art almost of necessity becomes its standard and its plummet. The artist cannot create Art until he has mastered the craftsmanship to utter it; yet even craftsmanship, which has certain limitations, is misunderstood by Criticism; and we get critics speaking of Style, meaning thereby the manner of some one else, a manner hallowed by tradition; whereas vital Style is the creation by the artist of a craftsmanship fitted to utter the desired impression most perfectly, and must be re-created for every work of Art if it be a consummate masterpiece—the which is almost exactly the reverse of what Criticism means by Style.

The artist has the right to use the tools of any man's craftsmanship, for the tools of craftsmanship are not Art. But no artist, whether poet or painter, may use the tools of craftsmanship to utter the filched vision of another man; first, because he is not uttering himself, which is the essential of Art, and secondly, because he has no right to thieve what is not, and never can be, his. The artist utters himself. The Brain-Thief filches the senses of another, or what he takes to be their senses, but can only filch the husk of such things; and filching

another's vision he endeavours to utter base coin—
he is without personality.

The history of the Art of man proves it. Let us
to the lesson of history, then, for him who has eyes
to read it.

All the Arts are one, and what is true of the one
is true of the other—but let us take the simple and
tangible Art of painting, the Art of vision, the
realm of which is the utterance of all sensation felt
through the sight, but the sight alone. All the Arts,
one in their intention, are different only in the
realm of impression in which they are born—painting has for its realm the impressions received
through the sight—music through the hearing—
and so with all; the limitation of the realm of an
Art is solely the limitation of the particular sense
through which it is perceived. Music, for instance,
cannot create the impressions of the eye, nor painting the impressions of the hearing. It follows that
the Arts of the vision can only be Art so long as
they create that which is within the sensing of the
eyes; and that the moment that painting attempts
to utter impressions outside the reach of the vision,
its intention is a bastard intention. So with the Art
of each of the senses.

Step by step, literature and the drama and sculpture have known the like onward impetus, the like onward sweeps of fulfilment, or intention of fulfilment—the like disasters—the like diseases—the like decay—and the like deaths. What do we find, written clear and precise, in the book of the past?

Art develops. Living Art is always development. The moment it ceases to develop it sickens and withers and dies.

STEPPING out of the mediæval years, the Italian painters essayed to find a new utterance—new in that it should express themselves and their age. They drew objects upon the wall. They then took to filling in their outlines with colours to give the general impression. Thereafter they sought to shade the objects like low-reliefs in sculpture. It took generations of genius to thrust forward the utterance of painting even so far. Then the Florentine genius pushed on, essaying to draw in perspective —as through Uccello. Then came Leonardo da Vinci and his fellows, who essayed to give *depth* by shading in some dark colour, and then colouring in with low general tones, to suggest the colours of nature, but without capacity to come closer to

colour than that. The Florentines, reaching their
supreme genius in Michelangelo, got little further
than this; but, mastering this instrument, they
compelled it to utter its fullest song. Thereafter
the Florentines were content to mimic Michelangelo and Leonardo and Raphael. In a generation
Florentine Art was dead; its craftsmanship alone
remained. Academism—the mimicry of other men
—had slain the Florentine genius.

In Venice, to the north, rising like a dream-city
amidst romance and splendour, painting from the
first essayed a far deeper and fuller utterance; it
sought to interpret the genius of the people in
colour. It early thrust itself far beyond the faculty
of all Florence. Step by step, but far more rapidly,
the Venetian genius found its way to song in
colour-orchestration, essayed to appeal in colour
lyrically to the sense of vision as music is employed
to the sense of hearing. A powerful chiaroscuro
was granted to Venice—the mysteries of dark and
light, from deep bass to high treble; she gave forth
revelation of herself in a wide gamut of colour.
From the years of Giorgione, to the end, she
moved towards colour-orchestration. But the giant
genius of Titian and of Tintoretto slew her—the

painters thereafter forgot to utter themselves, save
one here and there, and were content, nay strove,
to imitate Titian. Academism killed the Art of
Venice—as always it slays.

Then arose a rude fellow in Italy who flung all
the mimicries to the gutter, and went back to life
and the moods and impressions aroused in him by
the tragic intensity of things—his name Caravag-
gio—and founded the school of Naples, called the
Tenebrosi in that they enlarged the instrument of
painting so that the mighty shadows increased the
wonder of things and by their deep bass forced the
intensity of light. Out of these Tenebrosi—whom
the critics call Decadent, bless them!—came the
next prodigious conquest of Art through Spain
and Holland.

The Spanish genius, shackled though it was by
the Reason of the Church, arose in a vigorous realism—a frank and personal interpretation of the
life of the age—enormously increased the gamut
of utterance in painting through the deep orchestration of the Tenebrosi; advanced rapidly to the
mass-impressionism of the subtle Velazquez; and
he was scarce in his grave when the Spanish genius

died, blotted out in mimicry of the dead Italian masters—died of academism.

The Dutch genius—taking a longer time to mature, from the first intensely close in vision to the life of the people, unshackled by the classic tradition—compelled colour to its service, took up the revelation of the mysteries of light and shade discovered by the Tenebrosi, and went straight for mass-impressionism, bringing forth a galaxy of genius in Frans Hals, Vermeer, Rembrandt, and the rest. Yet, even as Frans Hals and Vermeer and Rembrandt wrought their wondrous Art, the eyes of the mediocre craftsmen and of fashion were turned by the writers to the Italian art; fashion flew to the Italianisers, and Hals and Rembrandt and most of the great Dutch genius died in beggary, to be buried in paupers' graves, whilst men of high promise, dreading the academic wrath, debauched their great gifts and fell to mimicry of Italy, which was not fit to untie the latchet of Holland's shoe. The mimicry of the Art of others triumphed—academism slew great Dutch Art as it has slain all Art.

France and England, beginning late, started in

mimicry, and looked well nigh like lost; but the
innate vitality of both peoples early threw off the
yoke. France was revealed to herself by Watteau,
and gave forth her delicate confession; and so we
had revealed to us France of the eighteenth century, through a galaxy of genius, Boucher, Fra-
gonard, Chardin, La Tour and the rest, who are
assailed by the critics because they did not paint
another age through the spectacles of an alien vision! the whole genius of France being in that she
uttered herself. England, uttering herself through
Hogarth, rapidly brought forth genius to state her
mighty adventure, until she stood forth in the
majesty of the supreme genius of Turner, who,
having mastered tradition, flung it aside and burst
forth in colour-orchestration such as had aforetime been undreamed of, and has been the revelation to vital genius into our own day. Putting aside
the allure of mere tricks of thumb, he compelled
colour to music, so that he won into our senses the
mood of the pearly dawn, the stillness of peaceful
waters, the roar of the tempest, the glory of the
sunset, the sweet-sad mood of twilight, the splendour of the ships upon the tide, the majesty of the
mountains, the reflection of mirroring waters, the

vast impressions of the eye. Yet even before Turner was laid in his grave, academism had puts its hands upon the British painters. Chilled by the classic academism of the day that tried to see England through the spectacles of Raphael and Michelangelo, but not realising the *why* of the chill, the Pre-Raphaelite Brotherhood went further back, and, in the name of rebels! they essayed to utter England with the voice of the primitives before Raphael. They held this to be "original," even whilst Turner was creating the vastest instrument known to painting before their eyes! This Academism gave birth to the Æsthetic Academism that sought through Morris and Burne-Jones to voice the England of their age in Mediæval-academism.

Meanwhile, France, awakened by England, had burst into song after the Revolution, and was gone out into the open fields. Taking up the instrument of painting where Hals and Rembrandt and Velazquez had laid it down, Manet led to Mass-impressionism: and the revelation of Turner brought Monet to Broken-colour-impressionism that the sunlight might come into French painting. But alongside vital Art strove the academisms. To-day the Primitive-academism has gone further back to Primal-academism, led thereto by Gauguin's return to the life of savage man; and painters seek out early Egyptian, Cambodian, and even Savage Art, and mimic these ancient Arts, with some vain idea that they are "original," forgetful that the Art of these peoples and ages is not only dead and gone, but that it was expressed in consummate fashion by the departed genius, and in such sincerity as can never be achieved by those who imitate them. This new form of Brain-Thief is just as much an academic as if he tried to thieve the vision of Michelangelo or Giotto. The critics—of course—wholly unable to grasp impressionism, have labelled this academism as "*Post*-impressionism"! A part of this academism, and linked with it —owing to the inability of the artists (who practise it) to grasp the basic intention of Art—is the dragging into Art various acts of the reason such as geometry and mathematics, called Cubism and Triangulation and the like. And, now, just as a vast increase has been made to the gamut of artistic utterance in painting, and it looked as if the Art were to come to fuller achievement in Colour-orchestration, we are afflicted with a new "originality" whereby painters are striving to utter our age in the realm of the vision which lies outside the range of the vision, and are creating a literary bastardy which is fatuously called "Futurism"— thus straining to tear an Art out of the function of the sense that alone produces it. If there were any relation between Art and the Reason, the Reason could convey far more quickly to the Intelligence what Art has to convey to the Intelligence; but it cannot be done.

It is the stupendous function of Art to reveal its age to the soul of man through the senses—a prodigious and eagle flight next to the adventure of life itself. What methods we employ matter nothing, so that the artist convey the compelling impression. But to go back to the vision of children or the utterance of the infancy of the world is but the dribbling of an idiot. He who would utter the vast and complex life of our age cannot do so on outworn instruments or by affecting the chatter of childhood. Equally certainly he will not do so by straining the function of one sense to utter the function of another. To give to Art the intention of science, and to essay adventures in geometry, cubes, pyramids, and the like, is to be-muddle Art with science; and however much sci-

ence may gain, Art will not be created—the senses
will know no communion of the impressions
aroused by life. But the falsity goes still further,
and the vision is asked to grasp what lies outside
its sensing—pictures are attempted in which sensations outside vision, such as take up impressions
through the hearing or taste or touch or smell, are
asked to join their alliance—which they cannot do.
The makers of this reaction are so barren in sense
of vision that they seek any conquest but the realm
of the vision. This is as bastard Art as the painting
which slops over into literature; or as though a
painting could not be understood without a barrel-
organ being let into the back, or the smell of a
string of onions being hidden behind it. The employment of a function outside painting, such as
geometry, is just as alien to painting as these things.
A sure sign of bastardy in painting is the need for
a written description to assist its intention or to
complete its impression. The range of impression
through the vision is colossal; and to ask the sight
to do the work of the other senses is to accuse it
of an insignificance and pettiness which reside
solely in the narrow brains of the accuser. To ask
the Art of vision—painting—to convey the impres-

sion of walking up and down a hill and smelling a
fried-fish shop is as though one blamed a man for
not preening his feathers. But, on the other hand,
*whatsoever impression can be aroused through the
faculty of vision is wholly and rightly justified in
the artistic utterance of painting.*

There is much cackle abroad to-day of Rhythm,
as if Art were Rhythm. This is a shifting of the
ground of the Brain-Thief from his old Beauty
fallacy. All the greatest masters have employed
Rhythm, ever since Art was. The Rhythm of the
Bible, as of Shakespeare, is astounding. It is no new
thing. It is as much a part of the battery of a
painter as are his paints. But an artist, if he desire
to utter Lack of Rhythm—as he must if he desire
to utter Violence—is as justified as if he desire to
utter Rhythmic things; and his utterance of Lack
of Rhythm may be as profound a masterpiece as
the other. The greatest Art conceals craftsmanship,
hides the machinery that creates it.

All that is most vital in the Arts to-day is concerned with Orchestral-impressionism as its instrument of utterance. It takes Rhythm in its stride,
as it takes every quality that aids it to utter the
impression desired with the most consummate

subtlety and compelling power. It never mistakes
Art for Rhythm, never plays with alien things.
All Art is the creation of the Imagination by and
through personal vision—and personal vision alone.
In its creation and utterance the Brain-'Thief cannot exist, any more than a jackass in the ocean.
It will come at last into its own. If many of those
of us who have practised it have had to live in the
desert—and the desert scars deep—the purifying
winds of the desert at least are about us, a purification that is as the coming of the sword to the academic, his withering and his humiliation. He has
filled your public galleries with small things that
have lost all meaning, and by God's good grace
has loaded the millionaires with the drift and waste
of infertile preciosities; by the accumulation
amongst the few he has near rid our age of the
dead, and thereby all unintentionally will rid the
people of false gods. His very thefts have been the
stealing of brass for gold, whereby he has cleansed
the house of the people—and Art abides with the
people and is their most precious heritage.

WHAT further need to follow the rise and fall
of Art? The slayer is always academism. Decadence

is always mimicry—insincerity—the Art of the Brain-Thief. The Brain-Thief is the filcher of the genius of another; had he the gift to create he would not need to thieve. The Brain-Thief is the assassin of Art.

In what immortal fashion Ibsen has drawn the Brain-Thief as filcher of kingship in *The Pretenders!* the tragedy of the man who steals the thought of another. With what skill he shows the born king of men in him who understands his age as against the hesitant bewilderment of him who gropes in tradition!

So the academic steep themselves in tradition. The new thought is ever the wrong thought to them—they are suspicious of life, resentful of vitality. For them, therefore, a code of laws built upon dead achievement. They, it is, who are ever for stoning the prophets. The bookish critic inevitably reads the laws, not the living Art—condemns or approves in the measure of the mimicry of past achievement, confident in wrongness, not realising that he is essaying to judge Art by what is the negation of Art. Inevitably he approves the Brain-Thief—for the Brain-Thief is lord of his realm. Inevitably he flings the jibe of Decadence

at Vitality, and approves as Vitality exactly what
is Decadence. Inevitably he is raised to high office
and power over the Arts; and the world blinks
and wonders wherefore Art withers under his rule
and administration. He fills the public galleries
with dead things; and all that is living and of significance he lets go by. He has always bowed down
to and worshipped the Brain-Thief.

The Brain-Thief is honoured by the State. He is
knighted and belauded and banqueted, and pours
forth his unwisdom. So Art gathers up her skirts,
buries her face in her mantle, and departs. She dare
scarcely speak—for the Censor; she is shouted
down when she speaks—by the censorious. The
Brain-Thief ever filches all the virtues.

Yet Art is the most vital function to a people
—more vital than parliaments or princes or bish-
ops or editors. It is the voice of Art that impels
the people to their highest destiny and to their fullest fulfilment. Without the Arts of oratory, of
literature, of the communion of the aspirations and
feelings of our fellow-men, we were little above
the apes.

When the people put Art from them and give
heed to the academic, the Brain-Thief is lord over

all, and the splendour of their race departs from them and goes to move virile breeds. So it behoves us to look well to it that we do not stone the seers.

For, mark it well, Art is no flippant jade that grins to please. Her weapon is Truth—not vulgar blatant truth, but spiritual truth. She shrinks no more from showing hideous things to be hideous than from showing beautiful things to be beautiful. Art is without fear; and woe be to such as will not give ear to her! The croon of the Brain-Thief is as the song of harlots; and the love of men is a fickle thing enough, and most easily snared. The voice of the mimic is a familiar sound; but the voice of Art may mean the strong discipline and rough wayfaring in desert places—and the Brain-Thief loves an easy bed.

Chapter XI

OF CRITICISM AND THE MILK OF ASSES

BY Criticism, be it understood, is not meant only the written word. Perhaps the worst, certainly the most bitter Critic, is the mediocre painter or writer criticising brother artists.

Nevertheless, Criticism is essential to judgment of achievement in Art. Every artist is not only a critic, but the very fact of his selection of means is an unwritten criticism. Criticism keeping its due function of service to Art is almost a necessity; but Criticism usurping the function of guiding others to understanding is a vain endeavour.

The artist must be a critic of his own endeavour —if a silent one; he is often the most brutal and narrow critic of the endeavour of his fellows—if not so silent an one.

We are all critics.

And we have the essential right to be critics; but we have as essential duty, in being critics, to speak out of our understanding. Criticism has no power to direct, to order, or to guide. Criticism has its useful function. It is a subordinate function and unnecessary to the creation of Art in so far as it is not the artist's own judgment.

Scholarship and the delving in the dust-laden records of Art shall avail the true critic nothing in his conception of Art. If he would utter criticism worthy for others to hear, he must array himself in the function and significance of Art alone—he must seek only in works of Art the one and only significance that is in all Art: *to discover what the artist has essayed to utter, and to judge whether the artist has achieved his desire.* And this apart from all Art of others.

The moment when Velazquez came to his milk teeth; what time Shakespeare lay him down and died; the age at which Beethoven put on socks—such things have naught to do with Art. A great work of Art is a great work of Art, whosoever painted it. If it be discovered that another painted it, or wrote it or wrought it, than he whom the world had credited with it, the work of Art remains just as great. To judge a work of Art by the reputation of the artist is mere intellectual snobbery.

The chief glory of the critic lies in that he may

encourage mastery—expose the charlatan—bring
vogue to the neglected. The uttermost that the
critic can do is to recognise—but let him see to it
that he first of all knows. For this is his only authority—that he shall know. And he can only
know in that he feels.

The gabbling forth, or uttering in print, of mere
personal opinions is not criticism.

THERE is no more dangerous enemy to Art than
the official critic.

Diderot, an honest and able man, in many ways
a noble one, set back and blasted much of what
was best in the Art of his age—brought hunger
and neglect to some of the supreme genius of his
day. For he mistook Art to be the pander to the
Encyclopædia—and Art shall not be shackled to
Education or Lack of Education.

Ruskin, an honest and a noble soul, set back and
would have suffocated and throttled the living
breath out of the Art of his day; would have
brought hunger and neglect to some of the supreme genius of his age—for he mistook Art to
be the page-boy to morality and the political econ-

omies; and Art is not shackled to Morality or Immorality.

Both men gave sanction to much that was rotten or inept; abhorred much that was good and great.

To-day, lesser men, rarely men of genius whatsoever, stepping into the shoes of these Great Dead, blindly essay to slay living Art, to narrow the recognition of Art to their own mean understanding, and bring neglect to the supreme genius of our age—for they mistake the aping of the Great Dead to be a part of Art. And Art shall not be chained in a grave-yard.

To-day the prig and the pedant triumph in criticism. They judge Art only by its craftsmanship, or have their eyes ever upon the old masters, forgetting that critics have in every age decried this very Art of the old masters when it was being created, as against the Art of a still more antique day! And Art shall not find itself in mimicry.

Criticism too often has usurped its function, and mistaken its province—its chief claim to power its ignorance of the real significance of Art—its chief pride its skill in the antique-dealer's traffic.

Not only do Critics judge the works of the living by the works of Art of the dead instead of by
their revelation of life—if critics of painting, they
study pictures and judge living Art by the pictures
of the dead—if critics of poetry, by the poetry of
the dead—if critics of the drama, by the drama of
the dead—if critics of sculpture, by the sculpture
of the dead—but to them must be laid the solemn
charge that the aloofness of the people, and their
suspicion of the Arts, is largely due by reason of
their everlasting cry that Art is only for a few.
The critics themselves mistaking Art for what it
is not, and, of course, claiming to be of the Few.

Neither Wilde nor Whistler, to name two men
of genius, could write with truth upon Art—yet
both men, when they allowed their instinct and
their sensing to take possession of them, created
Art.

Critics almost invariably approve of works of
Art according to their "artiness"—according to
their success in suggesting the artistry of the past,
not according to the vitality of their achievement,
the originality of their statement, their creative
force. Critics become so enslaved by the habit of
gazing at life through works of Art, that they

easily pass into a smug enthusiasm for their skill in gazing through the spectacles of others, the vision of tradition. Their pride is based in it. They take it for granted that no living artist can be as great as the great dead. Shakespeare's fellows were the last men in the world to realise that the supreme poet of the ages was drinking with them at the Mermaid Tavern. As like as not, they gave him lessons as to how to write drama between the passing of the bottle.

THE Artist is as a Mother bringing forth children to the fatherhood of the emotions.

Criticism is at best an eunuch that stands with drawn sword at the gateway of the Palace of Art, guarding the birth of Art—ofttimes guarding it that it may be born illegitimate; crying aloud for creation, but unable to create; demanding production, but impotent to produce; a loud thing of Emptiness, the child of Barrenness; clamouring for a harvest, but knowing not how to sow; calling for the gathering, but unable to reap; usurping the right to crown, but hard put to it to tell the bays from the dunce's cap. Criticism never yet created a work of Art, nor enabled a work of Art to be

created. Criticism never yet aroused in others the
sensing of Art. Overleaping his true function,
the critic becomes but the forger of fetters for
the artist. Yet every day he is given higher and
more authoritative place and power over the realm
of the artist—until at last he stands at the gates
of the Palace of Art, not understanding, blinking
bewildered at the birth of Art that is legitimate,
blaming it ofttimes in that it is not illegitimate.

The eunuch has no right to arrogance in the
House of Birth.

TO condone false Art and false endeavour in an
established Academy is a vulgar form of intellectual snobbery; but to condone false Art and false
endeavour in rival institutions to the academies,
especially when one is a member of them, is a still
more vulgar form of corruption.

NOW there is not the slightest reason why Critics
should be the abettors of the Brain-Thief—it is
simply an ugly habit due to the natural tendency
of a bookish man to judge the Arts, by bookish
theories founded on past achievement. Most critics
are absolutely sincere men—it is true that sincerity

in a Brain-Thief does not mitigate the theft, but
it at least signifies that if the Critic will only discard bad habits he may acquire good ones. The
power and influence of criticism to-day are enormous—far out of all proportion to its right—but
that is all the more reason that Criticism should
be sane. And Criticism can be sane—*if it will but
discover the basic significance of Art,* and judge
each separate work of Art by the power or lack
of power in the achievement of the artist in creating his intention.

The punishment inflicted on Ruskin by Whistler
has made Criticism nervous of being out of the
coming vogue. Critics swallowed the poison of
Whistler's falsities as greedily as aforetime they had
steeped themselves in the heady wine of Ruskin.

There is a widespread verdict: "I do not *like* this
or that"—as if Art were concerned with what we
like or dislike! The verdict that justifies a work
of Art is: "Am I moved by this thing? Has it increased my feelings and added to my experience?
Has it stirred me to conviction in its truth,
whether I like it or not, that the man who wrought
this thing has uttered his impression into my understanding? Has he done it with consummate skill

or blundering? Has he done it at all? Above all
—has he done it?" By the answer, and by it alone,
does it become *for us* a work of Art. If it shall not
reach our understanding, then *for us* it is not a
work of Art. How he does it, or fails to do it, is
another affair that has nothing to do with Art, but
is a matter of craftsmanship. The sole standard
for craftsmanship is whether it achieve Art or
fail to achieve. There is no copyright in craftsmanship; but there is this vital limitation, that the
craftsmanship for every work of Art must fit the
utterance of that impression, and not be, what the
bookish critics mistake it to be, a trick of thumb
of the artist. But it is an oft-proven fact that if a
man shall borrow too much of the craftsmanship
of another man, say of a Velazquez, he will also
come to borrow the spectacles and mimic the *Art*
of Velazquez instead of uttering his own soul. The
artist must make his craft anew every time he creates a work of Art, for every impression must
have a craftsmanship fitted to utter that impression, and that impression alone. It is clear that if
one would utter a solemn and tragic impression,
one's craft must take on a solemn cadence and
march with tragic bearing; if one would utter

blithe comedy, one's craft must jig to a merry lilt; so shall each impression know only an utterance fitted to communicate it into our senses and thereby conquer the imagination.

So pedants and professors have raised up their system of laws that they call Æsthetics. There are no such laws in Art—they are the Brain-Thieves' laws founded on the practice of dead artists, which is precisely death to Art. They have narrowed, indeed still narrow, the vast and mighty realm of man's sensing to the parish of the pretty and have made it the toy of a cult of prigs. They play with dead things; and swear that all other things are dead except their particular dead. Æsthetics, as a code of laws on Art, are a fantastic farce—they do not even cover past achievement, and are still more incompetent to cover vital Art as it arises. Every generation sees them altered and mutilated to fit, in as distorted closeness as they can with sophistry be made to fit, the revolutions which have proved their utter shabbiness. No man can grasp the significance of Art until he has flung the fantastic laws of Æsthetics, as created by the schoolmasters, on to the dust-heap. And it is well so. Æsthetics are the litany of the Brain-Thief.

THE cry: "Back to Nature!" has too often meant
the mimicry of Nature in colours or sounds. This
is a complete misunderstanding of Art, which is
not the scientific photographing of Nature. Nature
is not the aim of Art. Art employs the objects of
Nature as Life employs the Body, in order to realise itself, to express itself—to Be. The Flame cannot burn except in a vessel. The objects in Nature
play the part of the Lamp to the Flame, as the
Body is the lamp to Life. Without the Body cannot be Life; without the objects of Nature can be
no Art. That is All—but a mighty All. Simply to
reproduce Nature accurately in detail is not Art,
any more than to paint on a canvas is Art. A painting becomes a work of Art solely when the painter
communicates to our imagination what his eyes
have felt in the presence of Nature. This masterpiece cannot be produced by laws or rules of thumb
or "science of picture-making" or act of reason—
it is far higher than these; it is an act of instinct.
Nature is there; you cannot better the work of the
Creator.

But whilst Art is without limit and without law,
anything that a man likes to do is not therefore
Art because it is lawless and limitless. Criticism

has been shaken to its foundations of late; God is good—but Criticism is not going to become sane by rushing to embrace every form of trash simply because it does not understand it. Thus, when we see Criticism, shaking off its years of teaching, furtively putting away its old coat and suddenly jumping into the light with hot enthusiasm for everything that is new—good, bad, and indifferent— we do well to watch the Reformed Brain-Thief trying to say a new set of prayers in a new religion. He is the Brain-Thief still. He has stolen the new religion instead of the old—that is all. There is no maddest prophet but will find disciples just as sincere as the disciples of great and true genius; so it were well never to accept a school simply because it has disciples, until the school creates great Art; nor condemn a school merely because our ears are deaf to its artistry. To leap to homage of any fool because great prophets have been aforetime stoned is to be drunk with the milk of asses.

Chapter XII

OF DECAY

TO say that Art decays is as though one said that a man dies. Life dies in the individual; and Art dies in peoples. But Art as a function never dies, as Life never dies.

We have seen that Art was essential from the beginning of man; and will be as long as man endures. And as it was by power of intelligent communion that he rose above the brutes; so by that power alone will he rise to further fulfilment.

Nations rise and fall, peoples come and go, kings and heroes arise and vanish and their very names are forgot, religions grow and pass, but Life goes on and increases—and Art is thereby eternal and increases. Life in man can only know fulfilment through Art. Whether we like it or do not like it, so has it been ordained by our destiny.

ALL the Arts arise, flourish, burst into full song, and die. They are part of the eternal mystery of life and death. They have, by consequence, all the attributes of life and death. Born in life, rooted in life, they die as vitality passes. Their slayer is academism—always.

Since Art dies, it is become a fashion of the professorial and of the critical to put forth a system or science of Decadence, whereby is meant that the Arts become immoral, or are stricken with some vague disease of a rather naughty old age, or the like inevitable plague. And the fact that great artistic utterance is of short duration, and passes rapidly away, lends some colour to any theory. All great achievement in the Arts does pass away; but the cause of death of great Art in a people has ever been one malady—academism.

One of the most frequent fallacies about Art is that which accounts the painting of a nude woman as bad Art because it arouses the desire of man; but such being an innate and vital quality of man towards woman—its interpretation may be a stupendous, a great work of Art—it may not be a wise work of Art, but it is not of necessity a bad work of Art.

They that babble of Decadence are largely dull of comprehension; for they call that which is alive decadent—that which is decadent alive. There is

this canting catchpenny flung freely abroad that
naughtiness creates decadence in the Arts. But Art
has not for its aim the moralities or lack of moralities—naughtiness or lack of naughtiness. To the
devout of one devoutness the Madonna is a thing
to worship; to the devout of another devoutness
she is a thing of lesser significance. Again, sex is
a vital and majestic significance; yet men who filch
from their neighbours, who cruelly oppress others,
who lie and bear false witness and kill reputations,
will blush that others think they have known the
ecstasy of the love of a woman!

Where Art is wrought in imitation of dead Art,
there shall you ever discover decay; when it is
guilty of any insincerity, there is the stench of
decay; when it has lost its relation to life, it is in
decay; when it is mere mimicry, it is in decay;
when it strums the music of others, it is in decay.

The artist, or would-be artist, who deliberately
apes the dead Art of the past, is a decadent—the
true artist creates for his age. The Future no more
exists than the Past. What we would do we must
do now, or the years slip by and we are gone, and
in a little while we are as lost in the mists of

oblivion as though we had never been. Who knows
aught of them that raised their antique state and
called themselves great a few yesterdays of years
gone by? This everlasting hankering after immortal fame is mere dram-drinking. A heart gladdened
by your generosity and thrilled by splendid comradeship is worth the shabby "immortality" of all
the Emperors. The paint perishes; whole languages
die; marble falls asunder; the very cities are buried,
to become the foundations for the new. The greatest are so small. And you shall ever find that he is
the greatest artist who speaks in the tongue that
all may understand. The "limited edition" is a
farce; the little groups that preen themselves on
their superiority are so little. And be you sure that
he who writes such precious stuff that few can
understand, will never be understood, nor is worth
understanding.

The most vital, as it is the most difficult task, in
all Art is to create the fulness of the present, so
that the living may be partakers of a living splendour.

IT is essential to the artist to create the personal
expression of his age. This is what criticism almost

invariably seems unable to understand. The artistry of a Lely or a Kneller is attacked because it is not like the artistry of the great Italians, or like the artistry of some modern man. But therein lies its very splendour. The artistry of a Lely or a Kneller was fitted to express the age. It states its pompous age far more fitly, far more perfectly than the artistry of Michelangelo could have done. The artistry of Michelangelo would have been as fatuous in uttering the age and the Art of Lely or Kneller, as the artistry of Lely or Kneller in uttering the age of Michelangelo. That Michelangelo uttered his age more powerfully than Lely or Kneller theirs is another affair. It is when artists of another age seek to state their Art in the terms of Lely and Kneller that their Art dies; so does it when they essay to utter it in terms of Michelangelo or Titian. And the stench of its death is none the less vile because its decay shows the aping of Michelangelo or Titian.

MARK well, that in the highest form of being that Life has evolved for itself—the Human—the instincts, and even the very forms, of the lower developments through which Life has reached upwards, to arrive at him, *persist* in varying degrees. Man is evolved in every person by going through a rapid development from the lowest forms during the months of being born. And precisely the same must follow as to the quality of the Life that inhabits the body of Man during these lower stages. So we inevitably find that some men remain at lower development in their power to sense the fulness of Life than do others. In our natures are ever certain crude desires and instincts that would send us back to the beast. Base instincts are at constant war within us—quite apart from religious or moral attitude—to turn us back from Forward-moving, back to the lower intentions and spiritual content of earlier Man. The thief, the slayer, the religious bigot, all manner of criminality, may lurk in any man, waiting but for the opening of the door that shall let them loose. This degradation of the body, which is not a lamp of sufficient power to hold the larger flame of Life, plays a marked part in the decay of Art—and the trend backward of much Art-endeavour to-day to a lower plane of the utterance of earlier Man is very unmistakable. These academic reversions burst forth in cycles, and have always been.

IT has lately been written that "There is no decay" in the Arts. Of a surety there is decay. You cannot have life without death; nor flowering without withering. The writer, sincerely setting out with the noble purpose of championing modern Art, approves Mr. Balfour's definition of Decadence as being the "employment of an overwrought technique." This is the eternal confusion of Craft with Art. And it so happens that all primitive Art is remarkable for elaboration of technique!

But let us glance at another, who is accounted by no means the least of, and is more typical of, the journalistic writers on Art.

ART DOOMED WITHIN FIFTY YEARS
Startling Prophecy of Mr. George Moore.

Thus in the Autumn of 1912 the flaring bills of an evening paper.

Mr. George Moore had decided that Art was to die.

The editor seriously discussed this farce. It was considered sane enough for discussion. Mr. George Moore, we were solemnly assured, was a great judge in the matter. Let us take him seriously:

"We are at the end of the artistic age," said he

—*"we are not as far from it as from the Stone Age,
but the Art Age has ended as completely as that
of Stone."* Clearly Mr. Moore considers that there
has been a particular Art Age! As clearly there was
no Art in the Stone Age!

He proceeds to make it clear, *"so that anybody
can understand." "Nature is reality; Art is an in-
intellectual formula."* It unfortunately so happens
that this is precisely what Art is *not*. It will be news
to many that euclid and algebra, which are intellectual formulæ, are Art. However, it appears that
we get these precious "intellectual formulæ" *"solely
by segregation,"* for *"man is an imitative animal"*;
so that Art is clearly, to Mr. Moore, Mimicry; and
euclid and algebra were only achieved by segregation! However, if men foregather and isolate themselves into groups, they will produce through mimicry an "intellectual formula," which is Art! And
to prove this he asserts that *"we should have had
no Japanese Art if a shipload of Elgin marbles had
been wrecked off the coast of Jeddo."* However, he
adds that the decline of British Art was not due
to the Elgin marbles, but to the *railways!* so that
perhaps the Japanese would have won through
after all. Mr. Moore knows that it was the rail-

ways because *"they put nations in communication
with one another."* They evidently had not been
in touch before, but at any rate *"English Art was
insular; it had its own formulæ up to* 1850." Now
it happens that Turner, the supreme artist of the
British race, travelled all over Europe, and could
scarcely have ranged more widely even on railways. But, then, Mr. George Moore, having been
in Paris with Manet and Degas, "discovered" them;
whilst perhaps he has not yet discovered a far
mightier than they. Still, let us follow Mr. Moore.
*"You send a Japanese painter to Richmond, and
he brings you back a piece of Japan, and you send
an English painter to Japan, and he brings you
home a piece of England."* This sounds plausible,
but happens to be an utter misconception of the
function of Art. It is the sole province of the artist
to give us the impression that life makes upon *him*
and upon him alone. To miss that is to miss the
basic significance of Art; and Mr. Moore misses
it utterly. But in the very next breath he is saying
that to-day we cannot tell whether a painter is
English or Spanish or Japanese or Hottentot! It
would, however, appear that the Pre-Raphaelite
academism, a definite and acknowledged and

vaunted use of the spectacles of the Italian Renaissance before Raphael, the first serious reaction
against the supreme revelation of the genius of
Turner (which was a prodigious advance on all
former artistic utterance in painting) is considered
by Mr. Moore to have been a typically "insular
movement," that is to say, national vision! He so
utterly misunderstands it that he dubs it *"a new
formula"*—he evidently does not know whence it
came into England. However, it was one of these
precious new *"intellectual formulæ which are
Art"*; and they *"are not possible any longer"*!
Thank God. But what about the Æsthetic Movement? what about "Post-Impressionism" and "Cubism" and "Futurism"? These, according to Mr.
Moore's definition, would be Art, being *"new formulæ."* However—and Degas, we are told, shares
this fatuity—*"Pre-Raphaelitism was the last new
movement,"* because after that *"the French influence made itself felt."* Mr. Moore evidently does
not know that the Barbizon movement was inspired by Constable, and so-called "Impressionism"
in France by Turner; but that is a detail. It further
appears that British students got innoculated with
the *French "intellectual formulæ."* In fact, Mr.

Moore has come to the conclusion that since the
world is becoming every day more cosmopolitan,
and since Art is only a national intellectual formula, and can only be national, therefore there can
be no further Art because Mankind is becoming
every day less national! Mr. Moore naturally fails
to see that as Men are drawn more and more together, their vision must be vaster, and their Art,
by consequence, must be more prodigious.

It is quite true that as men lose narrow parochial vision their vision becomes more universal; but
why in Heaven's name this larger vision, which it
is the whole function of Art to create, should kill
Art, even if Art were what it is not, an intellectual
formula, it is difficult to discover. Why the Pre-
Raphaelite mimicry of Primitive Italian Art should
be insular and national to England, it is still more
difficult to understand.

If the Stone Age man could not produce Art,
yet was more "segregated," (presumably Mr.
Moore means more isolated in groups,) than the
more modern man, whose Art is due to segregation in groups—or why should Art cease in fifty
years because intellectual formulæ will cease, owing to railways or because Elgin marbles may be

wrecked on every coast?—but I give it up. However—

Asked the blunt Philistine question as to whether
it be a good investment to buy modern Art, Mr.
Moore further flounders. He evidently thinks that
mimicry of one artist by another is quite a modern
vice, due to the railways and easier communication! He proceeds to approve several brilliant artists—Steer, Tonks, Chowne—but forgets to men-
tion, or does not realise, far greater artists. He approves these because they paint *"beautiful pictures,"* not because they are creating vital revelation of their age. He never mentions the supreme
painters of the day. He probably does not know;
as he probably does not realise that Charles Keene,
for instance, created a superb Art, uttering the
life of his age in a fashion that sets him amongst
the immortals, even above Degas; he probably ad-
mires Manet and Degas for the very qualities that
have nothing to do with their greatness; he does
not realise that such men as Steinlen and Brangwyn are giving us the worker in the factory and
on the wharves and on our shipping, singing Labour with astounding power. However—

"As we wander over the world, seeing every-

body, we lose our artistic perceptions," that is to say we grow less able to create intellectual formulæ! Turner wandered over the world and increased his; and he is mightier than Manet and Degas and Monet and Whistler and Steer and Tonks and Fantin-Latour put together!

"*Art is a lonely thing.*" It so happens that loneliness is precisely what Art is not. The artist may and does often lead a lonely life—that is due to the ignorance and self-assurance of the gentlemen who write about Art—but he creates Art for the communion of his fellow-men, and communion is not loneliness.

It would again appear that "*there are artistic periods.*" How the ducks all jump on to the same pond! Mr. Moore seems to mistake the outburst of supreme artistic genius for the only Art. He does not realise that Art is being produced in every cottage, in every office, in the street, on the bus, everywhere at every moment, in its way as perfect as that of many of the gentlemen who think they are great artists. But why pursue this utter lack of understanding of Art and the basic significance of Art? If Mr. Moore does not see how "Post-Impressionism" from France can give a fillip to

British painting, how does he see Velazquez and
Hals giving a fillip to Manet? and Leonardo da
Vinci giving a fillip to John? and the rest of it?
Why deny the fillip to Britain and pass by the fillip
that Constable gave to the Barbizon man, and
Turner gave to the whole so-called "Impression-
ist movement" in France under Monet? What on
earth has the invention of a new intellectual formula to do with Art? It is for the artist to utter his
personal impressions of life—Art is that and nothing but that—and how he does it has no more to
do with Mr. George Moore's approval or disap-
proval, or with "intellectual formulæ," than with
spring onions or the London General Omnibus
Company.

"Nobody can appreciate pictures but a painter,"
says Mr. Moore, *"the public knows nothing about
Art."* Well, if the public does not know more
about Art than to please Mr. Moore, the world's
in a bad way.

So, *"in fifty years' time there will be no Art"*!
The poet and the painter, the sculptor and the ar-
chitect, the musician and the dramatist and the
novelist, the orator and the actor will have passed
for ever! And all because *"the painters who com-*

mand the highest favour in the salerooms to-day are the very men to whom Mr. George Moore pinned his faith so many years ago." Gog and Magog!

ALL these headlines and sound and fury signifying—nothing! In the whole of this wondrous "prophecy" not a word that reveals the very scantiest concept of the basic significance or intention or achievement of Art! nay, rather the mistaking of what it is not for Art.

Now Art, as we have seen, so far from being "an intellectual formula," is neither intellectual nor a formula. The moment it essays to be either of these things the life has gone out of it. Vast as life itself, illimitable as life, as long as man endures there will be Art. If nations pass wholly away, and the brotherhood of man become universal— whether kings or republics or communes shall govern all the future states—by so much as the brotherhood of man knows increase, by so much the deeper and wider and fuller will be Art, since without Art can there be no increase. If the dead thing that Mr. Moore mistakes for Art is to be more dead in fifty years, all is well. To deny Art to America because America *has no nationality,* is of a piece with Mr. Moore's academic thinking. America is as national as England is national, born out of the same origins, and destined to as majestic a wayfaring. We are own cousins to France and Germany and the Dutch and the Norse. America will give forth a prodigious Art, and has already brought forth singers. She is befuddled with the academic trash that Mr. Moore mistakes for Art; but she will cast false gods from her and emerge to utter an astounding artistry. Mr. Moore's prophecies are all the old quagmire of Æsthetics— an elaborate set of vague and contradictory theories and laws which are rotten to the core.

It is all of a piece with the academic idea of "patriotism" which vaunts the encouragement of small peoples to cling to their small language, not realising that thereby they are cutting themselves off from the wider adventure of the race.

Chapter XIII

OF THE DEALING IN ANTIQUITIES

THE labour spent upon dead Art to-day is prodigious.

To the dealer in Art-wares it is a legitimate business; it is his right and office to buy and sell curiosities, antique things. But it has as little to do with living Art as though he bought and sold any other beautiful commodity. Yet it is this very antique-dealer's traffic that is the basis and foundation of most critical writing upon Art—and is only too often the sole inspiration towards artistic endeavour in the studios. Even so honoured an expert as Dr. Bode uses the prices which pictures fetch at sale as a mighty argument of their artistic value!

There has arisen amongst us a solemn and wide cult that concerns itself with antique artistry. The value of a work of Art has come to rest on its rarity—the scarce thing. Dead Art is become the supreme significance of culture in the public aim. Museums are set up to hold it. Scores of clever men pore over books and steep themselves in the

study of dead painters, so that they become expert
in discovering who painted this and that. Vast sums
of money are spent in collecting what are called
"Old Masters"; and the buyers have some fantastic
idea that they are thereby concerning themselves
with Art. The thing they buy is, as often as not,
that out of which the significance and the Art
are departed, or are departing, and the craftsmanship alone remains. The ghost of the Past is revealed to us through them—that is their sole *artistic* value. Generally the men who are devoting
their lives and skill to this "experting" would not
know a vital work of Art when they saw it. And,
even in their antique-dealing, they are constantly
changing their opinions of the *value* of the dead
masters.

Many rich men, approving themselves cultured,
fill their palatial mansions with the artistic achievement of the past, who do not understand its first
significance. They even employ bookworms and
dealers and go-betweens to procure these works
for them, not trusting their own judgment! Their
sole anxiety is lest these things may be forgeries—
for they do not possess themselves of them for the
significance of the Art they hold, but because of

their rarity and value at auction. Their rooms are
like a museum, the walls hung with rare curiosities.
They would be hard put to it to explain the real
significance of these things—indeed, so would the
"experts." Ancient works of Art are torn from the
altars that they fitly adorned and glorified, and
above which they were once a significance to their
age; and these are set up in dining-rooms, where
they hang above the baked meats, ridiculous and
put to shame, fantastic and inappropriate, signifying nothing, making the home as unhomely as
a slaughter-house, as solemn as a cathedral, as mel-
ancholy as a police-court. Not only for good, but
for gaunt ill-drawn saints or forgotten incidents or
wholly unknown doings, painted by mediocre
Italian or Dutch or such-like primitive painters at
a period in Art when the craftsmanship of Art
was in a crude and inarticulate state, vast sums are
given, the buyers not realising what these things
mean, and the critics and experts not so much
concerned with the Art of them but squabbling as
to who painted them, and the need for vowing
them masterpieces because some clever fellow
amongst them avers them such and it would show
lack of culture not to agree with him—realising

still less that for moderate fees they might become possessed of far mightier masterpieces of living Art by far greater living painters. Suddenly they will suspect that a "masterpiece" by This One was by That—when its "value" at once drops! Ancient documents are ransacked to bring forth evidence as to the career of tenth-rate Renaissance painters whose Art, even when it was created, was an insignificance—and, being now wholly dead, is passed into further insignificance.

It were as though men, to prove their culture, gloried in ruins wherein to dwell; or made their habitations in ancient churches, or sat at meat amidst tombstones in a grave-yard.

AND as with the collectors, so with those who write criticism of Art. It founds itself on comparison with the Art of the dead; and its chief delight is Attribution. If the work of a living painter or writer be like the work of the Great Dead, then it is accounted great Art—if not, it is accounted Anarchy or an Impertinence or in some way inartistic.

This fantastic business goes coupled with sneers if a living artist's tricks of thumb be like some

other living artist's tricks of thumb; but a Raphael loses no shred of his splendour if *his* tricks of
handling be so like those of Perugino that the
critics and experts themselves quarrel as to whom
it was that painted certain masterpieces! Perugino
and Raphael both being reputed dead, both are
voted great.

Nearly the whole of this so-called Criticism is
based upon the antique-dealer's estimate of what is
Art, together with the pseudo-philosophy called
Æsthetics. By consequence we see real live Art
blossoming untended as best it may; or neglected,
as against the Art of the Dead; and the artist ban-
ished during the most splendid years of his career
into that awful isolation that is but too often the
punishment of genius. But let some mimic of any
antique craftsman, even of savage man or the infancy of the world, but paint in a manner that
bookish men recognise, then he is hailed as "original" and a genius.

SO Ruskin, a man of astounding genius in the
weaving of words into the Art of literature—a
master of Art in the making of prose—took upon
himself in exultant self-sufficiency to write of the

Art of painting—wasted his great literary gifts in fatuous and pompous pedantry on that of which he knew but little and sensed little. It came about that, in the province ordered by the dealer in antiques, he grew to wondrous skill in knowledge of ancient craftsmanship, and thereby won to honour as such amongst those that did not understand —thence he came to usurp the dictatorship over the realm of the Art of painting of which he had but limited cognisance, and thereafter to the lordship of the splendid acreage of the garden of the Arts, a very impostor—who, in his heart, detested imposture! And he needs no informer to bring him to judgment—he stands convicted of his guilt out of the words of his own mouth. For, the moment he stood before live Art—the moment he was brought face to face with the living thing, he stammered bewildered, jibbering, spluttering with the unrighteous anger of ignorance. Brought into the presence of the Art of a Whistler, he who had ever judged the living by the dead, lost his bearings—he had no light to guide, no "authorities" to give him aid. Living Art meant nothing to him; for he had no concept of Art's basic significance. This was bad enough; but, having the "cultured"

mob with him, he forthwith led it with much piety
to the stoning of the living Art. He added insolence to ignorance. To Ruskin the astounding
revelation of Whistler, and of the far greater men
of the school that had bred Whistler, meant nothing; it was but the "pouring of music into the ears
of a deaf man." The shallowness of his understanding of Art, all Ruskin's pseudo-culture in Art,
betrayed itself, violent and unashamed in the
presence of the new revelations. The subtleties,
the eloquence, the exquisite impressions that the
skill and insight of Whistler aroused in the emotions and gave forth in immortal fashion, were to
this blind man but the "flinging of a pot of paint
into the public's face"! How the fatuous words of
his guilt condemn him! And be it remembered
that wholly apart from his Art, had not Whistler
been gifted with a venomous and unscrupulous
wit, and employed it ruthlessly, he would have
sunk; and Ruskin's tyranny might have destroyed
further vital artistic intention in the British
peoples.

IF this were the sin of a poet of prose—such as
Ruskin—a master of the art of weaving words

into impressions, what is to be said of the multitudinous scribblers who essay to guide us into the
kingdom of the blind? who would lead us into the
desert of the antique museum habit, and leave us
there with the dead for companionship?

Dishonest? Not a shred. More honest men never
put pen to paper. But they have been trained in the
falsity that blasts all great artistic endeavour, and
glorifies all that is death to Art.

There is a profound and solemn assurance
amongst them that babble of Art that the Old
Masters, the Great Dead, have established the laws
of Art for ever. Scarce any suspect that these are
dead; or that the age they uttered so magnificently
has passed away. Nay, bewilderment and pained
surprise greet the very hint of it. To them it never
dawns that the Art of the Greeks was a live significance to the Greeks, but to us is a beautiful curiosity. From them it is hidden that the atmosphere
of Renaissance Italy was a mighty significance that
is gone beyond our breathing—its subtlety and its
reality largely departed from us—an affair for the
careful research of the student, burning much mid-
night oil—an air picked out of an antique instrument that yields but quaint, ghostly, half-under-

stood music to our ears to-day; of supreme value
in that it reveals to us something of a bygone time,
but utterly inadequate to utter our age.

To this antique-dealing bias of criticism the
whole conditions of the modern press, in which
these effusions must appear, add soil to make the
showy weeds of false Art to blossom and flourish.
The critic, if he speak out his judgment, may har-
ass the editor's advertisement columns—and it is
the curse of much modern journalism that, being
a commercial enterprise, it depends upon the vulgar commerce and traffic of finance. Should the
editor find his advertisements fall away, or receive private letters from indignant academic men,
who batten upon false art and grow to fame or
distinction and place thereby, the columns of his
pages know the critic no more—and the pseudo-
artistic critic takes the seat of judgment.

BUT that the antique-dealing vogue creates the
fulsome and fatuous follies of the "experts" were
a small affair; for the critics do not create Art.
The artists themselves are also debauched by following after false gods.

The studios! shall they cast all the blame upon

this criticism inspired by the antique-dealer's vision of the professor and the expert? Nine-and-ninety so-called artists out of a hundred are spending their lives essaying to achieve old masters, or to repeat the tricks of thumb of distinguished modern men. Did not wise old Constable thunder against and oppose a National Gallery, foreseeing this curse on Art? They set up some achievement of the great dead as a model, and essay to create a passable imitation of the work of his hands—they endeavour to state an idea, even when they would bring an idea to birth, as they think one of the Great Dead would have stated it. Their studios are walked by the ghosts of Pan or of Nymph or of Wood-gods or of Wine-gods, by Venetian grandees or Roman gladiators or old-world religiosities or Greek men and maidens. Yes, by Heavens, the youngster who paints a picture that recalls some primitive Italian or Dutchman is hailed as a "new light"—an original. Young sculptors are for ever carving or modelling modern antiques—as though, for all the world, they had never been beyond Saffron Hill. How many give hint even that they realise that the Greeks have created, once and for all time, in masterly fashion, far better and more perfect masterpieces in the utterance of the Greek spirit than we who are strangers could create their age—have uttered with consummate artistry the limited experience of their own epoch that cannot be surpassed by any modern, who must of necessity be an alien to that experience? Impressions that were a living significance to their age, that every shepherd in the Athenian dales could understand, in however limited fashion, require now a lexicon or a "book of the words" to explain them even to the cultured few and the alien of vision in our day.

The last thing that they realise is that the artistry of the past ages is wholly inappropriate to the present. The greatest compliment that can be paid to a mediocre painter in our midst is to tell him that his work is like that of Velazquez or Frans Hals or Another; it is the most resented stricture to a master.

Genius is not concerned with *appearing* "original"—it utters its sensing with all its power, and cares naught for all else. Artists too often read nothing but the effusions of academism, when indeed they read aught but the press-cuttings on their own works.

NOR does the evil influence of the dealer in antiquities end there. The master who is stoned arises and overwhelms the tyrannies that bade his stoning. But the deepest pathos of his triumph ofttimes lies in his very conquest; for the mediocre and the sycophant rush to his court and forthwith make of his mastery new fetters of tyranny wherewith to oppress the new generation—wherewith to gall the heels of the coming conqueror.

Even as Ruskin condemned the master-work of Whistler, so they that sat at the feet of Whistler, instead of reading the open book of his high achievement, inhaled the foolish words of his mouth, and now employ the whip of his weaknesses, his limitations, and his falsities, to scourge the younger masters who are arriving. And, as with Whistler, so with others. Yet it was probably by the venom of his mean squabbles that Whistler became famous to a wide public, rather than by the quality of his Art. And it is a pathetic comment on his many spites that every mediocrity to-day endeavours to set up a "personality" on a vile travesty of Whistler's insignificances rather than upon his superb and resolute habits as artist—they ape his paltry egotism and look for enemies

amongst their most generous allies, deeming themselves great in the measure of the brilliancy and
conceit of their treacheries! and triumphing with
shrill glee over a friend discomfited. Of a fool and
his folly, 'tis said by the gossips, there is no end.
Weeds spring ever apace in the potting-sheds of
the garden of Art; and with noisome efflorescence
would poison the air of its splendid acreage.

OF THE GREAT DEAD

THE National Gallery should be a lamp to Crafts-manship, a beacon-light to apprenticeship.

It is as often the grave-yard of artistic en-deavour, the breeder of intellectual hypocrisy and artistic snobbery, the debaucher of the nation's Art-virginity. There is no place in this land where more artists have committed Art's suicide than in the National Gallery; there is no land where more artists have done their careers to death than in Italy; the grave of the betrayed in the Art of France is dug deepest in the Louvre.

National Galleries should hold only the supreme masterpieces of man's achievement in painting—no matter by whom painted. They every day be-come subject to the mere bookworms and antique-hunters, who are concerned with petty pedagogic affairs quite outside Art, regardless of whether the work of Art be of supreme merit or the artist a supreme craftsman. For some fantastic reason the book-taught overlords of our taste value all dead

Art as of higher significance than the greatest
achievements of our own day. But the value of the
supreme work of Art is in itself alone; and its appeal is, and should be, its sole significance, whether
painted to-day or yesterday or in the centuries ago.

The creative artist, becoming possessed of the
dæmon to state his impressions of life, to utter his
sense of things felt, being compelled, therefore, to
create craftsmanship that shall give form to his Art
—to make the lamp in which the flame shall burn
—he at first, almost of necessity, essays to employ
the craftsmanship of the Great Dead, or something
akin to it. If he become enslaved by such craftsmanship to the Great Dead, his Art withers, or becomes stunted; he remains at best but an exquisite
craftsman, beautifully uttering nothing, or limps
along a maimed artistic life on crutches. A crutch
is none the less a crutch because it is beautifully
fashioned.

Now, it is necessary that our craftsmanship shall
become a confirmed habit before we may utter our
Art in all its perfection and fulness. The mind and
hand, torn and harassed by the difficulties of craftsmanship, cannot be free to concentrate upon the
statement of Art. The hand must be facile to utter

the thing desired, or the statement is halting and indeterminate. The lame may walk; but it is indifferent walking. Once the artist has conquered sufficient skill to utter his Art, his craftsmanship nevertheless is not complete—with each new effort he must increase his skill, and change his style to utter it fitly; even when his hand lies numbed in death, his craftsmanship will still be far from exhausted, and his desires incomplete.

That the student does well to study the craftsmanship of the Great Dead needs no wiseacre to determine. That the pathways to the utterance of Art discovered by the Great Dead make shortcuts to facility of craftsmanship, none but a dolt will deny. But that the revelation of the old masters, or of the new, holds as vast dangers as it holds aids to the student, is more rarely realised. For, the student, having learnt the lesson of the old masters, has to guard himself against stealing their vision; must see through his own eyes; and give forth the work of his own hands. And nothing lies heavier upon him, no shackles are more difficult to shake from him, than the fetters he puts on in the days of his studentship.

For in winning to skill of craftsmanship from

the example of the Great Dead, he is threatened ever with the danger of being tempted to lay aside his personal vision, and to drop into the facile habit of seeing life through the spectacles of the Great Dead.

It is the province of Art to interpret Life, not to imitate the interpretation of the dead—or others; not to mimic, but to reveal; to play the poet, not to play the ape.

ALL Art dies, giving place to new.

Yet not wholly dies—for the mightier achievement of the great Art of the past conveys to us something of the significance of the past. It is by and through the Arts of the Past that it is granted to us to increase our intelligence in so far as the Past can increase it. He who inhales from the spirit of the Art of the past something of this significance, is likely to be spurred to utter himself in majestic rivalry and emulation. But he who becomes enslaved by the mere forms of the past, is likely to become naught but a parrot or a slave.

All Art dies, giving place to new.

The love-lyric, uttered in the once music of the

Greeks that every shepherd in the Athenian dales could understand—since it was the living speech of his tongue and his pathway to communion— yields how little of its ancient fragrance even to the rare student who digs and delves with drudging toil in heavy lexicons to discover something of its hard-won significance to-day? Learned professors wrangle over the subtleties of its dead meanings, toiling to win back a little something of its essence that aforetime stirred, without rule of thumb or ponderous research, the quick ears of such as felt its lyric intensity but for the mere listening.

The Venus fallen from her altar in Melos, or the Madonna torn from her ancient state above the high altars of Italy, yield how much of the spirit and fragrance of their once significance into our senses who stand and gaze upon the wondrous skill of their exiled presence in some frigid gallery to-day? these things that held so mighty a meaning for them who bowed themselves at her feet in the solemn thrill of reverence in the years gone by, worshipping at their shrine in old-world yearning! Pan with his pipes of reed, Saint Sebastian arrow-pierced, and the multitudinous gods and goddesses and devils, all have passed or are passing—their once vast significance withered. Where aforetime they held a reality, in the cities that bred them, they are to-day but an exquisite curiosity.

Skill of craftsmanship in some measure remains; the spirit and the Art of their antique state are departing or are gone. The craftsmanship in part only; for these mellowed tones and pigments are no longer the colours that their creator wrought. *The false artistry of the academism of our day essays to repeat these beauties of decay, strives to create a dead language,* forgetting that the colours now embrowned and mellowed by age are but the splendid ruins of vivid hues long since vanished.

And why should it be otherwise? The beautiful in the dead passes away; but the ugly passes with it. The simple or complex faith that bred the Renaissance Madonnas of Italy, burnt and maimed and tortured its neighbour for lack of like faith. From the brutalities of the years when this Art was a significance we have travelled long leagues of forward journeyings, even though much that was fragrant and exquisite has departed with the brutalities.

AND if the spirit of Art that moved the Great Dead be flown, it behoves the student to guard himself against the dangers of becoming steeped in their craftsmanship, which was but the means whereby to utter their departed Art. That which the Great Dead did with consummate gifts, has been done once and for all, and may not be surpassed in its province. He who imitates can never surpass the thing he imitates.

Many a promising career lies wrecked upon the rocks of tradition that drew it to ruin at the very gateway beyond which lies the wondrous adventure of such as are dowered with the strength of genius to make the voyage upon the unknown and uncharted seas of artistic revelation. These wrecking rocks are peopled with such as lure to disaster by academic instincts; and have been themselves wrecked thereon—such as have wrapped themselves in the raiment of dead tradition and have worn the spectacles filched from the great dead; who have been content to essay utterance in a dead language; men who have been blind to the significance of their own age—and still more blind to the simple fact that all that is best in the past has been achieved by a mighty Art that can never be bettered by such as imitate it.

Of the many wise things spoken by Constable upon Art, none was more profound, none more far-sighted, than the phrase in which he laid down the verdict: "Should there be a National Gallery (which is talked of) there will be an end of the Art in poor old England, and she will become, in all that relates to painting, as much a nonentity as every other country that has one. The reason is plain; the manufacturers of pictures are then made the 'criterions of perfection instead of Nature."

Precisely.

The National Gallery to be of any value should contain only the supreme masterpieces of all time —above all, of our own time. Let the owners of pictures by the old masters sell their possessions to whom they will. It is of far more vital necessity for the good of Art that the finest living artists should be employed by the nation and by munici-pal bodies to create living Art, to beautify the public streets and squares and buildings, to en-courage by nobility of conception and exquisite-ness of understanding the aims and dignity of the people. The nation would do better to spend ten times the amount of every penny given to antique Art upon the encouragement of living masters. Think of the public buildings decorated by such a man as Brangwyn! Had his superb gifts been employed upon the interior embellishment of the Roman Catholic Cathedral at Westminster, it had become a place of pilgrimage to the Art-lovers of the world. Look at the interior now! Think of the treasure that such as Puvis de Chavannes laid up for municipal France! Consider the dignity that the works of such men bring to every place that they embellish with their great gifts. Think of a square holding the master-work of such as Rodin. Then go awhile and listen to the little men where they squabble over the little storms in their tin pots, where naught that is worthy is brewed.

OF THE ACADEMIC OF MIND

WHERESOEVER the academic of mind hold authority, you shall see this worship of dead things, this glorification of the beautiful dead husk of that which was once greatly alive.

It fell like a curse athwart the wayfaring of Whistler, of Manet, of the Barbizon men, Millet and Corot and the rest—it was the blight of the Scribes and Pharisees that galled the gentle spirit of the very Christ—it preaches death whilst it affects to preach life; and it is of its supreme insolence that, in preaching its death in life, it is most violent towards the genius that seeks life, but whom in the blindness of its self-sufficiency it cannot discover.

It is significant that it has ever essayed to waft its plague upon every fresh bursting forth of the tree of Art into leafage and flower and fruit.

YET it is inevitable that the Academies should foster false Art, indeed, that they should be fear-

ful of living Art. It is of the essence of Academies
to teach; as necessary to make laws in order to
teach; and, in this making of laws, to found them
on established achievement. Therefore, false Art,
the culture of the dead, has ever its stronghold
amongst the academic.

It is significant of the conceit of academism that
there should have arisen in our day serious persons
who have grown restive under the fact that Shakespeare wrote his plays. To the academic mind it is
unthinkable that the mightiest literary achievement of the ages should have been nurtured in a
little country town, and have blossomed to fulfilment in the garish atmosphere of the theatre—indeed, anywhere outside the academies. Whereas, to
such as are not pseudo-artistic, it were almost incredible that great Art could be born in the atmosphere of false Art—as incredible that a Shakespeare could have achieved his majestic Art had
he been reared and raised within the fold of the
academies!

He came, anarchic, trampling tradition under
foot; fresh from the meadows of Warwickshire,
the pure breezes of the free land fragrant about
him, the dews of morning upon his doublet; he

came flinging aside the conventions of the past, creating a mighty structure of craftsmanship for himself that he might give his vast Art its full utterance. For him the balderdash of Æsthetics not at all. To the academic men of his day he was a mere "Shakescenes." Even the greatest of them, whilst they owned to his splendour, apologised for him in that he had little Latin and less Greek! And we have seen pompous dullard after dullard in our day essaying to prove that the works of his hand must have been written by another—some other who had academic upbringing. The academic of his own day apologised for his lack of academism; those of to-day demand his academism. Stupidities have been piled on stupidities, raising a dunghill of pomposities, on which little men have stood and crowed their impotence. Senseless hands have been put forth to pluck Shakespeare from his own achievement.

Yet this could never have been for a moment but for the pseudo-artistic. No man with a real sense of Art would search for the bones of the author of *Hamlet* in Bacon's tomb, or bemuddle himself with fantastic cryptograms or childish zigzag puzzles, or disturb himself over Shakespeare's

lack of academic training—he would go straight
to the Art of the man and find that in no other
man's skill shall he discover kindred achievement.
The signature of an artist, whether poet or painter,
you shall not find in his written name at the foot
of his work—that were an easy affair for the forger
—but in the personal artistry that is the sign-
manual of the artist. To bemuddle the hand's skill
of Shakespeare with that of Bacon were as though
one confused the utterance of Turner with the
utterance of Corot, the utterance of Manet with
the utterance of Velazquez, the utterance of Wag-
ner with the utterance of Beethoven. But the colour and fragrance of words being more subtle than
the handling of paint, the pseudo-artistic at once
see the difference between the personal statement of
Turner as against the personal statement of Corot,
though in the years to come the majestic utterance
in colour of the little cockney son of a barber,
being so astounding in achievement, will likely
enough be challenged and attributed to Ruskin or,
Turner having been of the people and born in a
sordid alley, his works will be given to Disraeli or
D'Orsay—or the Duke of Wellington.

Those who spend themselves upon ridiculous de-

tails of Shakespeare's life in order that they may
squeeze them into Bacon's doublet, are unable to
realise that it had been as hard for Bacon to have
passed through the Latinities and pompous brain-
torturings of the academies and to have reached to
Shakespeare's ability and to have made Shakespeare's insignificant blunders, as for the camel to
pass through the needle's eye. Bacon's Romans
would not have fought with rapiers; but they
would have been less Roman.

Surely only the vulgarity of our age could have
brought forth such solemn dulness as would deny
to Shakespeare his wondrous artistry because he
had not been rendered barren by academic training
—only the vulgarity of the pedant could have
given the manifold blunders of Shakespeare's genius as being more likely to a swindling lawyer with
a liberal education!

GENIUS knows no class. It may step into the
palace of kings or the cottage of the peasant—into
the barber's shop to the lad who lathers his father's
shavelings or into the carpenter's work-shed, into
the garret or the manger; its sole law that it knows
no law; its chiefest whim that it is least likely to

enter or abide where wiseacres sweep and garnish their skulls to make it a dwelling-place.

In the academies, therefore, least of all; for the academies worship at the shrines of the dead. Whilst the professors make laws and dissect the withered flowers of the world's achievement, and essay to make a science of Art, Art blossoms elsewhere.

The academic breath blows dust over every living endeavour in the Arts. Indeed, has it not brought blight to the very meadows and gardens? For who shall feel increase of delight in a Buttercup as Ranunculus, or in a Daisy when it is pompously nick-named Bellis perennis? Who but thinks of pills when Dandelions pose as Taraxacum, or is thrilled with the memories of the sensitive plant if it be called the Flebottomoi hicoklorum? And as the enchantment of a garden loses its fragrance in the dog-Latin of the sciences, so do their fantastic laws essay to slay the vigour of our wondrous tongue with pompous Latinities mixed in a gluepot of Greek roots.

OF STYLE

STYLE is simply such perfection of craftsmanship as most perfectly utters the desired impression. Precisely as a musician changes the movement, key, cadence, volume of sound, and such-like qualities so that Music shall utter the mood desired, so it is absolutely the need of the artist in words or colour or the like to create a fit craftsmanship for every mood of impression that he essays to create and to pour into our senses.

There is, of necessity, a personal element in this craftsmanship, since all Art is an interpretation by the artist of the impressions made upon his senses. But many artists have caught a fine manner of stating an impression, which they proceed to repeat and employ thereafter for the expression of every impression, whether it fulfil the mood in the most perfect way or not; and almost invariably the critics account this false artistry of Self-academism to be Style.

Style, then, is the personal quality of craftsman-

ship whereby an artist gives form to his Art. Style
has no value in itself; and is sterile if employed as
its own object. All great Art creates Styles; since
Style must be created in order to give forth Art.

There is no word upon which the Academic batten more eagerly than upon Style.

We have seen that Ugliness has as legitimate
place in Art as has Beauty, that Tragedy and the
agonies of life are as legitimate a subject for Art
as Comedy or laughter—so, also, discords and violences are as lawful to Art as Restfulness and Harmonies. But Art must never be incoherent—it must
never lack style—the form and cadence and manner of handling must fit the mood, or the mood is
not created, and Art does not ensue.

It comes, by consequence, that the academic
mind and the mind that speaks of Art for Art's
sake, meaning Art for Craft's sake, naturally gets
to the considering of Style as the significant part
of Art—its end and object.

Perhaps the saddest example of this falsity was
Flaubert, the prophet of Art for Art's sake.
Prophet of a creed which he himself but half-
believed, he essayed to write a prose as precious
as verse, he racked himself on the wheel of Style;

he made of Style a torment, a plague, a joy of
strenuous aim; he tore his days to pieces searching
for the absolute word, seeking the exquisite shade
of nicety in a phrase; it was his religion, his god, his
idol. And at the end of all came the confession of
the revelation: "What distinguishes great geniuses
is generalisation and creation: they . . . bring
new characters to the conscious perception of humanity . . . Shakespeare is something prodigious
in this; he was not a man, but a continent; there
were great men in him, whole crowds, countries.
They have no need of attending to style, men like
that, they are strong in spite of all their faults and
because of them; but we, the little ones, we are
worth nothing except by finish of execution. Hugo,
in this century, will knock the bottom out of
everybody, though he is full of bad things; but
what a wind! what a wind! I venture here to say
what I would not dare to express elsewhere: the
great men often write very badly, and so much the
better for them. It is not to them that we must go
to look for the Art of form, but to the second
bests, to Horace, to La Bruyère. . . ."

Walter Pater glorified the "chiselled phrase"; but

Walter Pater had so scant idea of Art that he essayed to make the living speech of his own age into
a dead language. He it was who committed the
much-coo'd fatuity that Art should "burn with a
hard gem-like flame," and called it "an ecstasy"!
As though a flame were hard or like a gem; or the
quality of burning were hardness or gem-like! As
though the qualities of a flame were not rather
the very opposite of hardness, and far from the
rigid essence of gems!

It is this very pedantry, this schoolmastering,
that is the cause of decay, when indeed it is not the
cause of lack of birth, in all artistic endeavour.
Dramatists go to the Great Dead, as do painters
and writers, poets and decorators, to find inspiration. But he who would give life to the drama shall
walk rough-shod over the graves of the dead. For
him shall be no digging in grave-yards, no refur-
bishings of ancient things. The race to-day would
hear that of which our forefathers never even
dreamed. The very crowd has arrived at the gates
towards which our forefathers but peered. It is
for the artist to create, not to revivify what is gone
and what was better done in the past.

The Arts are not the children of the academies. Let the dead bury their dead.

The pose of artist is a modern affair, with its roots in the long-haired untidy habits of the early Victorian Bohemian, evolving through the clean pretence of these once genuinely dirty habits, and ending in our own day as the self-sufficiency of a little conceited class apart—above all other beings —in a consequential piddling superiority that proves the so-called artists to be ignorant of the whole significance of Art. These affectors of the artistic cult are an absurdity; and the man in the street does well to have a healthy contempt for such.

Critics speak in praise of a Style because the author, painter, or poet, or whatsoever artist he be, is to be recognised always by uttering all things in a like manner. The moment the desire for Style overmasters Art so as to express in colour, phrasing, or cadence, the mood of laughter and gaiety in the same manner and tones as the mood of solemn and tragic things, Style is dead. It is the province and value of Style that the creator shall employ a different Style to utter different moods.

Yet, to-day, the very men who write a novel

in the one dry cold measure that the critics call Style—largely set up from translations of French and Russian masters—are just precisely those who are hailed as Stylists, for the very reason of their incapacity to realise vital Style!

Chapter XVII

OF THE LAW

LAW is a necessity. The Law is founded in Thou Shalt Not. For there is need of Thou Shalt Not, that good order may prevail—that by our acts we shall not conflict with our fellows.

But that is the sole virtue in the Law.

Law is sterile; it cannot create; it can but prevent. Its function is to prevent.

Life is a great Thou Shalt; and it is Thou Shalt alone that advances Life.

It is the province of Art to create—to increase the sense and experiences of Life—for Art is the emotional revelation of Life, the Increaser of the acreage of the garden of Life.

The academic of mind, the critic and the pedant, are given to look upon Art as an affair of law. The laws of Art are the veriest crutches of the halt. No work of Art can be created to laws. Art is not a science. The discipline and the guidance of an artist have this severity: that no rules of thumb, no ready-reckoner, no recipe can create a work

of Art. The artist has to create the craftsmanship
that will evolve each work of Art fitly. When the
academic talk of the laws they mean precedent, the
acts of craftsmanship of tradition—the which were
employed by others, but which have no function or
right for the use of any other artist.

There are critics who set Art to the service of
morality. But morality is not created by laws; you
may only guard against immorality by laws.

Art is wholly independent of morality or of immorality as its function; Art can create that which
offends against morality or that which supports
morality. And it is a significant fact that the Art
which breathes the forward-moving revelation of
life is generally attacked by the very people who
preen themselves on being moralists; whilst these
very moralists will often as not accept without de-
mur the basest forms of Art.

For Art can be base as well as noble. What is
more, the craftsmanship of base Art may be as perfect as the craftsmanship of noble Art.

The artist may be a pander to the basest instincts
of man, with astounding powers of artistry, as
Beauty may be a very prostitute. The Art of pleas-
ing may be the pander to things of unutterable

shame. Amusement may give forth shrill laughter
to the most ignoble ticklings of the senses. And one
of the worst dangers of our present day—a danger
that threatens wide and appalling disaster—is the
passing of the function of the public Press from
the desire to appeal to the noblest sentiments and
to lead the public taste, into a mere commercial
vulgarity the aim of which is to make wealth by
following the baser instincts of the lower part of
the community, by mistaking the mob for the de-
mocracy, by "giving the public what it wants"—
a sinister and vile phrase that covers the basest
hypocrisy disguising the harsher truth that the
public will buy what is provided by the lower
taste of those who cater for its baser desires. This
base traffic in the lower passions, which of a truth
we all have, is hidden in a cant of conventional virtue. Every sentiment is degraded into a mawkish
fulsome sentimentality. And as proof of the wide
heritage of our mawkish and vulgar tastes, we see
the panders growing wealthy upon their traffic—
and we find the journals that give forth this sensational and sentimental stuff widely read and widely
bought in vaunted "largest circulations."

And, God! if men would only exercise their

imagination and look upon some of the demi-gods
who there dictate in wise anonymity our people's
opinion, set the standard of our taste, and rouse
our baser senses! Cockney or Levantine, or British-
born, they approach a work of Art, whether painting or literature or drama, solely from the view
of the sensational or the payable. How can Art
flourish on such a dunghill? or how a people be led
to the majestic conception of its destiny? What, to
them, is the forward-moving of the race? They
hold but one estimate of the splendour of life—the
weight of all endeavour, of all ambition, of all
significance, is only gold. They employ the battle-
cries and phrases of the forward-moving and the
noble to cover their ignobilities; they assail with
grave faces the calling of the harlot and the thief
and the bearer of false witness, who, poor souls,
for all their baseness, mostly but sell their worthier
selves for that very same gold which is the others'
hire. The million are content to let their ideas and
estimate of life be created for them by the printed
word in these sheets, who if they but tore aside the
veil that screens the writers, would wonder at their
servitude. Yet the million, by letting these base
things into their home, become partakers in their

shame, and come away tainted and lowered—for all that is best in the million is tricked with the phrasing of the nobler battle-cries, and pay into the tills a fortune that goes ever to increase the treasury which mints the false coin for their further lowering.

Chapter XVIII

LIBERTY THE BREATH OF ART

LIBERTY is an essential to the creation of Art. And if Great Art must be unfettered by laws that it may arise in the land, much more must it be wholly freed from Censorship—if it shall lead the race to the heights and be a lamp to sovereignty.

Yet every vulgarian is out against the Liberty and Might of Art.

The chief excuse for all such Censorship is ever the Improper Book, the Indecent Play, the Immoral Picture, and such-like cant that readily rises to the lips of the self-adjudged Respectable. Afraid of Life, they fling their lean arms about the feet of the more vigorous and the upward-climbing to keep them with them rather than let the more virile others rise above them. Being mediocre, they naturally worship mediocrity. Being fearful, they batten on Fear.

Whether there be Censor or no Censor, there will always be indecent and vile works of Art. It is a fantastic fact that Censors nearly always reign

187

over periods where vileness is most rampart, and
Art most mediocre.

When a people are given Liberty, it is a strange
truth that by their very Liberty they are cleansed.
It would seem a logical danger that the more Liberty a people are given, the more dangerous a
weapon of misuse is put into their hands; but it is
human experience that, on the contrary, the dignity that ensues to a free people brings a more
stately concept of life that kills the danger.

From whom, then, does the clamour for Censorship ever come? Always from the traffickers in the
Arts. You shall find in the theatre that the slavish
love of censorship is ever the desire of the traffickers of the stage—the man who runs the shop, the
man who is there to make money out of it—not
the artist who creates the drama.

You shall find in literature that the slavish lust
for censorship is ever in the traffickers of books—
in the circulating library—in the shopman—not
in the artist who creates the literature. These
Censor-mongers form themselves into "associa-
tions," "societies," and the like. Their last thought
is of Art or the welfare of the artist. It is always

money-getting, or cant, or some pettifogging desire to curb Art to their petty concept of strangling
life.

But a people who permit any body of vulgarians
to come between them and their Art are unfit for
great Art or a great destiny. They have the ordinary laws of decency to protect them; they have a
hundred and one ways of blotting out the product
of base artists; and if they do not blot out such
works by the chill sneer of neglect, they alone are
to blame for it. Many a great artist would be condemned for immorality by some one. The Bible
contains chapters that are loathsome to the most
hardened palate. It would be impossible for a
writer of to-day to publish novels like the thirty-
eighth chapter of Genesis when we have no Censor
—for the simple reason that literature is free, and
the public has no stomach for such things. Yet,
surely he is an utter fool who would thrust into
punishment the printers of the Bible—one of the
most majestic works in our tongue!

To-day amongst circulating libraries they censor
books because one or two rather vulgar volumes
have been published. Can the self-righteous men,

who are combining to censure literature, come out
in a body before the public, and, before usurping
the office of censor, assure us on oath that they are
free from sins far more vile, each one of them?
Will they affirm that they have been guiltless of
mean or vile acts against their fellows more black
than the sins they condemn even in such books
as all decent men condemn? Have they never
jockeyed a partner, nor betrayed a friend, nor done
a soul-scorching injustice to another? Who are they
to stand before the world and decide that this artist
or that one shall die with their Art unuttered?

And what is to be thought of a people's manhood that will allow a gang of tradesmen to dictate
to them what they shall read? Are these men so
intoxicated with their self-righteousness that they
forget that they are but traders whose sole province
is to buy and sell books—that it is for the readers
alone to decide what they shall have or not have?
A people so lost to all sense of liberty as not to boy-
cott and blot out the tyranny of the cant of their
tradesmen over their intelligence, deserve to be
robbed of the splendid heritage of the garden of
Art; and they shall be filched of it; for a people
get the tyrant they would suffer. And not the least

irony is that the mawkish sentimentality that it is permitted only to the "young person" to read, is so untrue to life that the young person goes out into the world as shorn lamb to the raider.

Chapter XIX

OF AUTHORITY AND THE LAW-GIVER

THE weak ones, of us Humans, love to run about and discover some deep-baying mouth that shall set up for us a table of the laws that we may bow down and worship—and thereby rid ourselves of adventure—securing restful freedom from responsibility. And it is fit and meet, if we would thus depute our Will and our Personality to the deep-voiced Baying One, that we should set laurels in his hair; but is our splendour thereby increased?

Our morning paper makes our opinion for us. But has no man in a hundred the imagination to pierce the veil and discover the Little Thing on the high stool that chews the end of his pen and creates these opinions? Would the ninety and nine hug their cherished "opinions" so rapturously if they once saw the creator of them in his inky-fingered reality? Does the inky-fingered one never look into his mirror?

Should we accept with as unctuous bend of the neck the wisdom of an emperor on things in gen-

eral thundered forth in a steel cuirass, gay feathers
in his hat, if he spoke them in his night-shirt?

AS I blot these lines, Mr. Arthur Balfour has de-
livered his Romanes Lecture to Oxford upon
Beauty and the Criticism of Beauty. . . . You
see: they are all bitten with it! For it is abundantly
clear that by Beauty our statesman means Art.
. . . Yet Mr. Balfour has pressed further towards
the real significance of Art than most writers have
done—much nearer than any Slade Professor of
Art. And could he but have shaken from him the
loaded falsities of centuries and the atmosphere of
the academies, he might have given us one of the
most weighty pronouncements upon Art ever
spoken. He confesses that Criticism has been a
hopeless failure. He laughs at the folly of the
tyranny put upon critics by ancient critics—even
whilst he himself employs the word "æsthetic" in
its bastard sense of the science of the Beautiful,
instead of its original Greek sense of "feeling." He
boldly threw his genial contempt upon the academic making of laws for any Art, the futility of
thinking that Art could be created by laws, the
fatuity of making Art subserve the ends of morali-

ties or religion or the like as its function, the falsity
of allowing training and study the right to decide
or dictate what was Art, and the over-rating of
mere technique as against the real significance of a
work of Art. So close he stepped to the unlocking
of the gates of the garden of Art! But at the very
threshold he trips over the skipping-rope of the
professors, and falls—he who had come so near to
the whole revelation. Then comes the old old burden under which we have been borne down for
centuries! So he must harp on "a beautiful work
of Art" as the end of Art! With a loud bang the
gates of the Splendid Wayfaring slam in his face;
the keys have been snatched from his fingers. He
seems to think that whilst the critic is not justified
in claiming morality or religion or the like for the
ultimate function of Art, he must claim Beauty as
its function! But then he half regretted his con-
demnations, and he ended by reaffirming the falsity
that Art had "no ends except the æsthetic feeling
aroused by the beautiful!" He even came to the
question as to "whether society was better for Art's
being pursued." Well, if by Art he means the beautiful, it is not better nor worse. He repeatedly betrays that he takes "æsthetic pleasure" to be the

aim of Art; thus blotting all great and tragic Art from the world's achievement—since that which is intended to produce horror or pity or the agonies or tragic emotions is false if it produce pleasurable emotions.

And the dear delightful Academics gurgled—as though they turned sweet wisdom, jujube-like, upon the tongue. There was "Applause."

Thus it was that, even as he uttered the great truth: "if the Emotion was the real matter they had to discuss and consider in estimating a work of Art": he missed the truth by testing it in terms of "enjoyment," blundering into much whimsical logic-chopping about "discrimination growing, but sensibility not growing with it." He stumbled at times on so rich a phrase as "æsthetic appreciation" (appreciation of the sensed thing), but unfortunately he did not mean it, but rather the pleasure derived from beauty. This he proved by speaking of "æsthetic emotion," which is only another way of saying "emotional emotion" or "sensed emotion," unless you drag in the bastard academic meaning of æsthetics being a science of beauty. Thereafter he walked in the accustomed academic tangle as to Anarchy, and showed deep respect for

the German philosophic effort to include Art in
their "systems"—quite unwitting of the fact that
German philosophy, like most other philosophy,
has never understood a tinker's trough about Art,
but only buzzed ponderous solemnities about
"pleasure" and "beauty" and the rest of the pretty
jargon.

It is quite true that, if German philosophy had
been right as to Art being beauty or pleasure, the
burden thrown thereby upon Art it would have
been "impossible for Art to bear." But Art is far
more important, far more significant than anything the German philosophies ever dreamed it to
be. Had Mr. Balfour, however, or the German
philosophers, realised that Art is our only emotional means of communing with our fellows—our
sole means of communicating our sensations to
others, and therefore as important as Speech—then
they had strained their "systems" no shred beyond
their utmost capacity, nor had Mr. Balfour gazed
on Art with doubting heart of St. Thomas as
merely a pretty business, nor have denied the importance of its splendour or its unbreaking power
to bear any burden.

Thus it came about that Mr. Balfour went on

to draw distinction between the emotions—where Art draws no distinction of disparagement or pedantic classification—which he called "emotions that do not move to action and emotions that do"; and thus and otherwise ended in an academic morass of "subclasses" and folderols and other professor's jargon, for all the world as if he were dissecting butterflies or collecting postage stamps; all due to this falsity into which he had stepped about Art and Beauty.

Nevertheless, Mr. Balfour has given us one of the finest essays on criticism, marked by all too rare insight and courage, possible from a man to whom has not been revealed the full significance of Art—baffled by the academic falsities that he courageously strove to rid from him but could not. He failed, signally failed, as he was bound to fail, since he mistook the whole significance of Art for its pretty skirts; even whilst he came almost within entering into the splendid acreage, his fingers on the latch of the gate, but baulked by the wrong key.

Mr. Balfour has an idea that this is an age of Science, and therefore destructive to Art! He could not trip into such a bog, covered though it

be with treacherous and seeming grass, did he but
grasp that no age can live without Art—that man
without Art cannot live except as the beasts of
the field.

AMIDST a prodigious flood of works written di-
rectly with the intention of explaining or discovering the significance of Art, by philosophers, professors, critics and the like, none come so near to
the full significance as two works by *creative
artists:* Tolstoy's *What is Art?* and Shaw's *Sanity
of Art.*

There have been marked signs of an endeavour
to clear Art of its many confusions; and if abor-
tive, only so because critics seem unable to rid
themselves of academic falsities. Sincere scholars,
giving their lives to the business, have done prodigious service to the archæological and scientific
survey of dead artists, though such things have
little to do with the basic significance of Art. It is
inevitable that successful research should lead these
scholarly men to go a step further and pour forth
laws and rulings upon Art. Let us glance at "expert" criticism, so-called, of the most widely in-
fluential type to-day.

The archæological researches into the history of painting in the Italy of the Renaissance in particular has of recent years been profound: and one of the most brilliant students of that achievement is Berenson. The same may be said of Dr. Bode concerning Dutch, Flemish, and German painting. Yet, step aside from scientific interest in the Italian achievement, and consider the significance of their Art, and Berenson at once betrays faulty perception. He not only flits from one standard to another as the measure whereby to judge significance of Art, betraying unrest, though his sincerity urges him to strive with intense eagerness to discover the real significance; but at times he employs a phrase that reaches so close to the significance of Art that his instinct would appear to guide him to wonderful appreciation. But he lacks the full vision, and the significance eludes him again. He cannot rid himself of established conventions, which a good grasp of the Oneness of all Art would make him shed from him. Over and over again he rightly questions the oneness of Art and Beauty, but only to fall into the falsity again. He cannot bring himself to forsake it for all his keenness of mind. Even when he rids himself of Beauty he puts Enjoyment in its place. But one does not *enjoy* tragedy or tears or sorrow.

Berenson opens his interesting volume on the Florentine achievement with a phrase that made one think he had discovered the reality of its Art as wondrously truly as he has tracked down the tricks of thumb of its painters. But he forthwith proceeds to invent theories of craftsmanship with hideous names such as "tactile values" and "retinal impressions," which make the teeth ache; and which, when they are true, did he but essay to create a work of Art, he would soon find to be the elements of their industry for which students have the simplest terms. A theory of "tactile values" sounds learned to the ignorant. A few months' endeavour to create Art in painting would have taught him that the Florentine development of painting consisted in the simple fact that the first essay of the painter to create Art on a flat surface is to draw forms in line—then to fill in the forms with colour—then to create the illusion of depth, just as the flat surface of a mirror contains the aërial deeps of the atmosphere reflected therein round and about objects—in other words, to show things in the round; and one at once finds that the means to do this, so that objects look as if you could touch them, is to reproduce the light and shade upon them. To give these simple five-finger exercises to the world at this time of day in serious authoritative manner as a great discovery is fantastically pompous.

Berenson uses terms like "pleasure" and "enjoyment," but hesitates, and proceeds to give such terms meanings that they have not got, but which he employs to suit his theories. He created a stupid phrase, "space composition," which no artist would use, and which is opposed to an artist's meaning of the word "space"—yet the groundlings love it. By it he simply means composition that creates depth. But after all, this jargon matters nothing; it is all an affair of craftsmanship, and has nothing to do with Art. This effort to set up "pleasure" as the basis of Art, is made to include "displeasure" it would seem. And it is small wonder that, having built up the function of Art on the grave falsity of the giving of pleasure, that Berenson condemns one of the great portraits of the Early Renaissance, Andrea dal Castagno's swaggering swash-buckler Pippo Spano, *because* it "descends to mere swagger"!

Dr. Bode is another scholarly authority on the scientific attribution of antique artists, who, the moment he essays to write his impressions on their Art, reveals the limitations of his perception of the significance of Art. And perhaps nothing has done more to shake the public faith in all this expert antique-dealing than the gorgeous farce of the so-called Leonardo Bust—from which we gather that if a work of Art be by Leonardo it is therefore worth thousands of pounds and is great, but if the same work be by Mr. Lucas of Southampton it cannot be great, and is worth as many pence!

Then there is the Sentimentalist who prates of Art being Praise, which sends an even greater number of masterpieces into the ditch. There is, thank God, no limit to the vastness of the domain of Art. Art can dispraise as well as praise.

NOW as to the Professors, the teachers of students. Two professors have lately given forth books, hailed with solemn approval by critics. The one called his work *The Science of Picture-Making!* so, as the negroes tersely put it, " 'nuf said." The other called his volume *Art and Life,* but as it was

chiefly given up to the lauding of all that is Death
to Art, again " 'nuf said."

Thus they will confuse Art with anything. The
religious man demands of it—religion. The Moralist—morality. The Immoral Man—immorality.
The Craftsman—craft. Anything but Art.

Then there is the Pseudo-Scientific Criticism
that confuses Art with Science, particularly with
Disease or Lack of Disease. The most brilliant of
these was Max Nordau, who, in his book, *Degen-
eration,* which had an enormous sale, and a wide
and serious vogue, looked upon Art from the win-
dow of the Hospital for the Investigation of Crime
and Madness.

Lastly, we come to what we may call the Type
Critic of the Press. Mr. George Moore wrote in the
'nineties certain books, collections of Art-criticism,
phrased with remarkable vividness, which for a
time had wide influence upon his fellow-critics of
painting. To show how far such works carry, I
have repeatedly found Mr. Moore quoted with
awe-filled pen by recent writers. Now, Mr. Moore,
when he yields himself to the impression created
upon his sensitive personality by a work of Art is
often quite illuminating. But the moment he

theorises upon Art we find him repeating clap-
trap. I will not here go into the many falsities of
his theories, such as that Art is created by the
genius of a people in decay—indeed, was it not Mr.
Moore who held that the number of syllables in a
man's name affected his genius?—and the rest of it.
He has probably long since repented of these in-
discretions. He would never have evolved all this
stuff if he had realised at the time the real and vital
significance of Art. The Isms were in full blast in
those days. Mr. Moore was typical of the journalistic critic, who never thinks of testing the theories
about Art, but simply champions some vogue.
Now, "values" had become a kind of religion in
the studios; and of course the critics talked "values." But how shallow was Mr. Moore's conception
of Art at that time we may discover from a phrase
which has been repeatedly quoted by critics to this
very day. Said Mr. Moore: "By values is meant the
amount of light and shadow contained in a tone
. . . and Corot excelled in that mode of pictorial
expression known as values, or shall I say chiaroscuro, for in truth he who would say values has
hinted chiaroscuro." Now it is almost unthinkable
that a man who would seem to reveal in his writ-

ings so subtle a sense of colour and form as does
Mr. Moore, should so bemuddle the thing called
"values" by the painter—for, had he made the
simplest essay in painting, one of the first problems
he would have had to face, one of the first problems a lad who has been painting for a few weeks
has to face, is values. Values, it so happens, have
nothing whatever to do with light and shade, called
"chiaroscuro" by the Italians. Chiaroscuro is the
relation of light and darkness in a painting—what
artists call the "black and white" of it. By colour-
values the artist means the relation of colours, the
one to the other, as modified in the vision owing
to their distance from the eye as changed by the
depth of atmosphere in which they are bathed.
Perhaps it is best to define it by example. If you
take a white handkerchief and hold it against an
equally white wall or door, you will find the colours of the two things are exactly the same—that
is to say, they are the same "value" of whiteness.
Step back half a dozen paces with the handkerchief
in your hand, and hold it up before the white door,
and you will find that though both are still the
same white, and in the same light, the whiteness of
the distant door looks quite grey beyond the now

more intense whiteness of the nearer handkerchief. In other words, the "values" have completely changed. The volume of atmosphere between them has changed their "value" of whiteness. Let Mr. Moore try to paint white daisies in front of a white wall, and he will soon discover "values."

Chapter XX

OF THE RECEIVERS OF ART

AND you, for whom Art is created in heavy labour, if you shall not be granted the faculties to sense a work of Art, then pass it by, like an ignorant strong man, reverently, but without lip-service. Have no shame. You have but been denied the splendour—that is all. Some of us must be poor. Neither Criticism, nor the jargon of criticism, shall arouse in you the sense to see that to which your eyes are blind, to hear that to which your ears are deaf. At best it will arouse in you but an hypocrisy —a pretence of sensing what you do not feel— therefore a lie.

But in such measure as it shall have been granted to you to feel the emotions of Art, and in such realm of Art to which you have been given the key —go to Art hungrily to increase your infinity of fine feeling; and as your soul and your life grow larger thereby, your senses will grow keener, as fine steel increases sharpness by contact with the grind-stone where dull metal falls away to further dulness of its edges. Once entered into the garden of Art you shall know no backward crawling to dull places. To him who knows the vastness of pity, life can never again be lived in the once narrow pathways; to him to whom has once been revealed the majesty and the splendour of life, the creak of the parish pump of petty endeavours will call in vain. And it is the glory of the artist that he can bring the splendours into the cottage or the palace. It is of the fantastic laughter of the immortals that to the university and the academy are ofttimes forbidden the largeness of experience in the majesty of the emotions that is known by some who have slept with the night-sky for their blanket, and been victualled upon the north-wind of neglect for their harsh supper.

YOU shall only know Art according to the degree of your desire and the sensitiveness of your understanding. No talk of others, no guidance of pedantry, shall lead you thereto. He may only receive Art who seeks it in simplicity and sympathy.

And of them that receive Art, the range is as though one climbed towards a height, seeking on the heights the largest experience of life. And as each one climbs, according to his capacity, he reaches at length to that rung or degree above which he can climb no further—and understand. All that is vaster and mightier above him he has not the eyes to see nor the understanding to feel. To him that highest rung is the topmost limit of his climbing. The achievement to his level he feels and to it his senses respond.

If he be a consequential fellow, he will deny further heights and rail at them. If he shall have climbed in reverent spirit, he may suspect the Beyond; even if the stars be outside his comprehension he will suspect that there are stars. If he be petty of soul, he will there seat himself and deliver himself of judgments, denying the Beyond, content with his level, sneering at those below.

Chapter XXI

OF SUBJECT

ONE of the most pronounced pieces of cant blurted forth by the pseudo-artistic is the sneer at "subject" in a work of Art. No work of Art is without subject; but there is false subject—the sort of subject that it is the province of one Art to utter better than another, and which when attempted by the Art less fitted to express it overbears that Art.

A painting is so limited in its area of time and space that it is wholly unfitted to tell a story which requires time and sequence, the which faculties are wholly denied to painting. The canvas that attempts thus to state that which requires time and sequence, or any form of continuity, must fail as a work of Art. The nearest that the Art of painting can approach to action is to seize a significant moment of a drama and state it—even so, it fails in Art if the statement be not in itself complete—in other words, if the pictured thing require any explanation whatsoever outside itself. The dramatic picture is, therefore, an intensely difficult form of Art. The "Futurists" are perfectly within the realm of the Art of painting when they essay to show action, as long as that action is within the range of vision; they employ an utterly bastard Art when they essay to compel painting to express what the governess was thinking when the postman called.

Art is not concerned with immorality any more than with morality, with Ugliness any more than with Beauty, with lack of religion any more than with religion. The whole gamut of the emotions is its wide empire, but the emotions alone.

It follows that if one's emotion be "moral," the Art will sense morality; if one's emotion or feeling be "immoral," then Art will conduce to immorality. But morality and immorality are shifting affairs; what is morality to one generation may be immorality to another. Morality is an affair of the intellect, and Art has no concern with it as Art— for Art is an affair of the senses.

Great Art is the achievement of the mood of the thing sensed, whether moral or immoral, whether beautiful or ugly, whether amusing or serious, whether religious or lacking religion. *Bad* Art is the failure to produce by fitting craftsmanship the mood desired.

Noble Art creates the noble emotions; base Art creates the ignoble emotions—but both Arts, in order to create these emotions, must be "good" Art, or they fail to create anything.

Clearly the sole limit of the subject of an Art is that it must come within the range of the sense that creates that Art—painting must be limited to what is sensed through the eyes—music to what is sensed through the hearing—and so with the others. Whatsoever is dramatic has just as much emotional excitement upon us as what is undramatic. But to deny a subject to painting aroused in our senses by reading literature would be to deny almost the whole achievement of the Italian Renaissance, of which a large body of the masterpieces were illustrations of the Bible.

A philosophic idea, however it may appeal to our intellect, cannot become Art until it is turned into terms of the senses.

Let us take the Novel, which is the creation of character by means of story: To create a Romance or tale of adventuring, it is the aim of Art to thrill

the senses by action. To create the larger Art of
the Novel it is the aim of Art to create character
moving to the action of drama. But simply to tell
a story does not create the Art of a romance; nor
simply to label characters does not create the Art
of the novel. It is essential so to employ words
that the action of romance or the reality of the
characters is made to live in our senses. The
printing-press pours out so-called novels and ro-
mances by the thousand to-day, which are but the
feeblest attempts of Art. The writers have no
capacity to employ words except in the crudest
manner. The same rhythm, the same monotonous
dry statement, the same empty phrasing, the same
cadence or measure of words, where indeed there
is any attempt at rhythm or cadence at all, are
used to state the merry peel of wedding bells, the
solemn pomp of the stately funeral, the sordid life,
or the splendid wayfaring. Whether the winds ride
like mad devils over the blackened heaths, or the
sun climb over the golden fields, whether there be
laughter or weeping, such writers have no skill to
pour these emotions into our senses by skilled use
of words, but are content to appeal with dry

grammatical phrase to our thinking alone—they
tell us that there is a storm at sea, but we feel nothing of the violence.

There are schools of Realists who build up vast
structures of scientific facts; there are Art-for-
Art's-Sake men who play with phrases that are
cleverly put together and tickle the fancy with a
hundred delightful affectations but have no creative power to compel upon our senses the sensations desired. There are ninety and nine schools,
and manias, and rule-o'-thumb pluckers at the
strings of the mighty orchestra of prose or verse;
every scene, every movement, every chapter is
stated with precisely the same clever trick or lack
of clever trick; every mood is uttered in the same
measure, poured out in the same monotony of
rhythm, lack of colour and cadence, and with mere
bald intellectual appeal. Whereas the true artist
employs every means that skill can devise to usurp
our senses and compel our feelings, to make us experience the reality of life, to thrust into our companionship the children of his imagination, to make
us one with him in the moods of experience, and
to impel upon us the impressions of living—each
mood changes the music of words that fit its phrase

and utter its significance—when the earth smiles
with gladness, his words skip to a blithe cadence;
when the solemnity of the mystery of death chills
the heart and walks over the land, the phrasing
takes a different measure and the colour of the
words goes into mourning. The senses answer in
tune to the large gamut of his artistry, whether
tragedy grip at the capacity for the agonies of life,
or comedy fill the air with laughter. He tunes his
lyre to the majestic impressions of a sublime emotion, and has the skill to employ the lighter lyric
moods for lighter lyric moments. He is a master of
his craftsmanship; and being the master and creator of a Style that fits his subject, he flings to the
prig and the pedant the laws that tickle their little
souls but would be a fetter to his large wayfaring.

The supreme artist in words, in all time, was
Shakespeare. He wrought with words, weaving
them with supreme mastery, at an age when English was at its richest, most tuneful, and most col-
ourful. And with what astounding skill he creates
with a few phrases the sensations aroused in us by
the fragrance of the meadows; as in the blithe lyric
measure of "when daisies pied and violets blue, and
lady-smocks all silver-white, and cuckoo buds of

yellow hue, do paint the meadows with delight!"
With what sublime dignity of cadence he rouses in
us the majestic mood; as in the immortal realisa-
tion, by means of words, of man's imagination:
"Like the baseless fabric of this vision, the cloud-
capp'd towers, the gorgeous palaces, the solemn
temples, the great globe itself, yea, all which it
inherit, shall dissolve, and, like this unsubstantial
pageant faded, leave not a wrack behind. We are
such things as dreams are made on, and our little
life is rounded with a sleep!"

The academic mind is wont to look upon Poetry
as verse. It is but a part of the confusion of Art
with Craftsmanship. Some of the mightiest poetry
has been uttered in prose. Verse and prose are but
the craftsmanship of Art, are but the forms in
which Poetry arrays itself. For Poetry is the Art of
Words. As the emotional statement becomes more
exquisite and tense, the words to create them are
inclined to fall into more rhythmic cadence, to
pass even into rhyme that increases their music—
in tense moments the human emotions burst into
song, and utter themselves lyrically. In that degree
poetry becomes verse. But verse does not create
poetry—and is often wholly lacking in it. Rhymed

Poetry best utters itself in lyrical outbursts; long-sustained rhyming is most often the murderer of Art. But rhythm and a subtle cadence are a part of prose; as present in prose as in blank verse—even though it wear more subtle raiment.

Indeed, where shall you find verse that uttered poetry more exquisite than the prose that the great translators wrought in the pages of the English Bible?

Out of the genius of the Jews has come down to us through the Art of their great literature high artistic utterance. "They that go down to the sea in ships, and have their business in great waters, these see the works of the Lord, and His wonders in the deep."

Chapter XXII

OF THE BREED OF THE CONQUERORS

NOW, Dominion in the world goes to the Master race.

The Master race is that which has the will and discipline to live the fullest life without debauching it, or enfeebling its strength by excess.

The lamp of the Masterfolk is the highest Truth —its soul the noblest Instinct—its need the number of its splendid companions.

As the race evolves, it has to increase its strength, and to grasp still newer and vaster Truths, reach to larger ambitions, live mightier sensing, array itself in more vigorous endeavour. It must live a larger life; or it must fail in the strife for mastery, and fall away amongst the lesser breeds—be swept into the lesser places of the earth.

What was the truth and thereby guidance to our forefathers has won us our inheritance; but, being ours, has ceased to lead us to further goals.

You shall not find the new truth by delving in old books for it. The new truth is for ever being born. See to it that we have the strength for the new truths.

The New Truth comes pregnant with guidance towards a wondrous destiny—seeking to change the face of the world.

But just as Life cannot realise itself until it take a body to itself, so Thought is wholly barren and futile until it can transmute itself into a reality by clothing itself in the human emotions.

We do not live a Thought by *thinking* it—it only becomes a part of life when we *feel* it.

The greatest thinker is of no avail unless we live his thought; that is to say, unless we live it by personal experience, or it be transmuted into Art by an artist, who, by changing the thought into an emotional statement, thereby transfers it to our senses so that we, too, feel as if we had lived it. A thought that cannot enter experience is as though a man were given a birthday present of the North Pole.

The professor, with dandruff on collar, can state a solemn truth that two and two make four, or that a man shall love a woman or the race perish. Yet he leaves us cold. It is when the artist, by his alchemy, makes the truth a living thing that leaps

into our senses, that the great Thought is quickened in our emotions, thrills the blood, nerves the
will, urges to action, and sets the heart aflame—so
that it becomes a beacon-light to our voyaging, a
bugle-call that sends us jigging towards heaven or
hell—careless of death, reckless of the eternities.

Behind us is the rotting Past; before us the
Splendid Wayfaring over a wider world, through
a larger experience, that we may know a fuller life
—the New Truth leads thereto, but the New
Truth is blurred and tangled amid a myriad
chimeras of unlivable things, and it is given us by
Art to test the reality or unreality.

THE spirit that animated ancient Greece and Italy
and Spain is departed, the breath has left the dead
body. Their aim, their ideals, their attitude, their
vital significance are no more. We may look upon
the loftiness of their ambitions, the splendour of
their ideals, the high intention of their nobler
achievement with admiration; their Art hands on
something of immortality in these; but in its fulness and in its intimacy we shall never know it. It
has passed for ever. A new age has dawned—a new
generation—that needs new lamps for its beacon

light, new ambitions for its forward moving; that feels differently, sees differently.

Even the sublime Art of Shakespeare, already growing old to the aims of our more complicated age, will one day become an affair for the patient student, its language will pass into an unspoken tongue—its significance to be torn from it only by hard effort.

The old Art can never be the new. Its tongue is a foreign tongue; its utterance is the halting speech of an alien breed. To listen to it is to strain the hearing, and we but half understand; but living Art leaps into our understanding. An interpreter should not need an interpreter to interpret his interpretations.

No scholarship, no drudgery into books of explanations can yield us the sensing of the artistic thing. Art leaps into our senses, finding a welcome home therein, creating the answering sensations—or it fails to stir and is wholly withheld from us.

YET the achievement of the Great Dead is not without its inspiration and its significance. For our schooling of studentship we may learn much, must avoid much, through the travail of their wayfar-

ing. If we realise the spirit in which they wrought,
and remember that they employed their craftsmanship to create an Art that has passed, their
achievement is a lamp to our feet to teach us to go
and do likewise and create a craftsmanship fitting
to our artistry.

But let no man think he has come to freedom
and found himself, until the lessons he has learnt are
put behind him, and he has discovered his own
means to express his Art fitly. It is not till he rises
from the school of tradition that his Art shall find
wings upon which to soar. It is not until he has
thrown off the splendid tyranny of his masters and
utters the emotional statement of that which he
himself has felt that he becomes himself a master.

Suddenly, almost unconsciously, if he be a creative artist, he awakes to find that he has mastered
the tools of his craft, that the means whereby he
utters his Art renders what he desires—awakes to
find that he needs no longer to bend his whole wits
on the handling of his skill of treatment. Only
then can he utter his Art with fulness; only then
can he burst into full song.

Most men are, in their degree, artists. All men,
in their degree, are moved by Art. All men are able

to receive Art, each according to the measure of his sensitiveness—save only such as walk in the kingdom of the mad; nay, even such must be a very nullity, sans vision, sans hearing, sans taste, sans everything.

THE supreme artist, 'tis true and inevitable, arises but seldom. Genius is rare. That is why dullards and prigs and pedants ever mistake rarity for genius.

It is when his creative faculty bathes itself in the sheer joy of impressional achievement that the artist utters himself alone. Skill of statement, ease of utterance, facility with the tools of his craft, must have become a confirmed habit. Then only does he brace himself to his sovereignty—discipline himself for high governance—when he is master of his craftsmanship, so much master that he can attune his Style to the idea that he would create. It is the ecstatic moment in which he takes the mystic sacraments of coronation. He knows that the sceptre of empire over the realm of the imagination is given into his hands; and, with the candour of the conqueror, he accepts it, knowing the power that is behind his throne; knowing that he is no shabby puppet wearing the mantle of his betters; knowing, too, that his life must be the keen-eyed struggle of the usurper to keep that throne. . . . The age of his crown does not make a king's significance; it is in the kingship within the skull beneath it.

There is now a wondrous music in his utterance that the world has not before heard—a perfection of statement that the world has not before seen. Some magic has fallen upon the vision of the man; and his skill of hand leaps eagerly to express that vision and utter the poet that is in him. Thenceforth his craftsmanship states emotionally every impression that he desires to express. What has rent the veil and yielded him the mysteries, he himself, maybe, could not put into precise words, mayhap does not fully realise in terms of thought; the whole significance is in that he has felt overwhelmingly, and his hand's craft has by its wizardry been enabled to utter what he has felt.

Chapter XXIII

OF SPLENDID REBELS

THE artist must be of the breed of the conquerors. He has to discover a new world. As must all who would reach to majesty and dominion; to reveal, the artist has to break the table of the outworn laws. He must create a larger law—a larger law to fit a larger purpose.

The artist creates his Art; and in the doing he creates Style to express that Art; Art creates Style —Style cannot create Art.

Revolution! Such is ever the cry of the hidebound. The Commonplace Man utters the word with rounded mouth of awe. But Revolution is the Conqueror's sword; and little men may not wield it, or they perish. 'Tis the hewer of life to the master breeds.

The New Vision, which leads to man's forward-moving, must ever challenge current morality as well as current and established things that stand in the way of forward-moving, and forward-moving ever appears insane or blasphemous or anarchic to the mediocre. And to add to their fear, they confuse what is virile and forward-moving with what is futile and fantastic in the dreams of false prophets.

He who revolts before his race is ripe, must die for it. But the race, being ripe for forward mastery, will move to mastery like a Youth stepping into his heritage.

You shall mark how the Commonplace Mind leaps like a frightened thing to spit forth the nickname of Anarchy when his littlenesses are assailed. The bewildered mob leaps forth from its anarchic home and rushes forthwith to cast stones at "Anarchy." But the man who is stoned or starved or assailed as Anarchist to-day is like enough to be enshrined as demi-god to-morrow.

The new revelation towards the heights is ever anarchic to the hide-bound. The giver of the New Law looms ever anarchic to the followers of the Stale Law; for he breaks the Old Law and shatters it. To the form-ridden Israelites, the Mightiest of the Jews loomed anarchic; the Scribes and Pharisees assailed the Christ as Anarchist, and they crucified Him for it—for indeed He was anarchist to their anarchy. To the Roman soldiery and to the Scribes

and Pharisees, the Christ was the breaker of the
Old Law, for He created the New. Yet, to this day,
the preachers preach from the same pulpit the
Old Law, An eye for an eye, and a tooth for a
tooth, and the New Law, If thine enemy smite
thee upon the one cheek, hold out the other. Aforetime they ordained that man should love his neighbour as himself, and straightway burnt him to jus-
tify their neighbourliness in desiring his salvation.
So give they forth the Stale Law and the New Law
in the same anarchic breath, and suspect no foolishness, yet are filled with a bewilderment of wonder that they who sit at their feet keep neither
law!

So through the long ages, the Maker of the New
Law looms ever anarchic; so every leader of our
forward-moving is ever assailed—in Art as in all
else. And the mob, being fools or dullards, stones
the maker of the new laws; and having stoned him
and becoming conquered by him, straightway uses
his new law as a whip to scourge those that come
after him who would enlarge his law and increase
his revelation.

Every tomfool bewails anarchy in Art—too
dullard to see that he was but bewailing life in Art,

that anarchy has naught to do with the business
except that his own anarchies and confusions are
being flung down.

THE living artist must dig his hands deep into the
hearts of his fellows. It is for them alone that he
may light the lamp of his genius. He is there to
reveal life to them—to reveal themselves to themselves. His function is to come to mastery by supreme service. In so far as his Art reveals a wider
life to his fellows, in so far he is conqueror. By the
measure of his failure to reveal life is the depth of
his failure as artist.

The artist must give forth the new atmosphere
—he may be stoned for it; he may have to live in
isolation to utter it; his dwelling-place for years
may likely enough be the desert of neglect. His
calling requires that awful and august solitude of
misunderstanding during his best years, even amidst
the roar of the traffic of his fellow-men. But if he
see the truth and utter it fearlessly, his will be a
great reward.

It is God's aristocracy who are crucified.

And the appalling part of the awful sacrifice is
that the revelation of the crucified is taken up by

the narrow of skull, and is debauched into a creed that shall be a whip to scourge the future crucified.

THE artist is the increaser of Freedom. And it is the splendour of Freedom that the Free Man creates *for himself* the great discipline, *for his fellows* a larger tolerance. No man shall achieve freedom, save by self-discipline. It is the emblem of the Slavefolk that they would win to licence by fettering their companions—for the very Freedom of the Slavefolk is a meanness.

And if you shall not have the courage to make larger and fuller the life of your brethren; if you shall shrink from the desert, then back to your counting-house, so that your money-getting be fair honest industry. Keep at least the Splendid Wayfaring from uncleanness. Be the lesser thing handsomely.

For—and mark this well—'tis a lonely thing to be an artist.

THE THEATRE AND THE PURITAN

THE THEATRE AND THE PURITAN

WELL! well!

There sat of late, solemnly—mark you, not in a theatre of farce, with faces grotesquely painted to make the world giggle, but called to their serious business by the State—a Royal Commission of august personages to judge whether there shall be a Censor of the Art of the Theatre—the vital Art of the Drama! And whom did they examine? The Censor as defendant of his fantastic usurpation on the one hand; and the playwrights, the creators of the drama, on the other? Not a bit of it. Were such the sole clear issue, there were scant need for a Royal Commission to discover a fatuity. The creators of the drama know full well that they cannot create great and living Art with full powers if jacks-in-office, and the champions of dead conventions, or academic minds, are set in power above them. For no man may walk upright if loaded with fetters and chains. No great Art can be created by slaves. No; so lacking were the judges in the knowledge of the significance of Art, that the whole trade of the theatre was called in. By consequence, the vital issue as to whether or not the Censorship mars the creation of great and noble Art—the only question worth talking about—inevitably resolved itself practically into the question whether the traffickers in the drama were benefited by the Censorship, which does not in the least matter, since the tradesmen of the theatre have no more need for dry-nursing and protection than the sellers of fried fish. It appeared, however, that the Censor did not even protect morality with overwhelming success! And a particularly dry fact emerged: that the trade of the theatre dreaded the censorship of public opinion more than that of the Censor! O Morality!

At least we had the privilege of seeing the critic of "the first newspaper of the world," standing before the nation, speaking of the function and aim of the Art of the drama as being "an evening's æsthetic gratification"! Is the demigodish pronouncement of such, that all Art is "over-rated," out of place in such thinking-machinery?

What have half these witnesses to do with Art? Why not call in the wig-maker, the ice-cream man, the girl who serves behind the refreshment bar, the fireman, the scene-shifter, the lime-light man?

He who creates the Art of the drama is the dramatist. The players of his plays come and depart, and others play them. But the dramatist struck down, the drama ceases. He it is who creates the significance. On the dramatist the Art of the theatre depends. And it is the dramatist who can be gagged and fettered and reduced to mediocrity; or, in being freed, can create the living Art; it is through him alone that the wings of its majestic ranging may be clipped, and brought to the gutter, or nailed to the shop's counter.

AT a gathering of men concerned with, and employed in, the activities of the drama, there chanced awhile ago an after-dinner debate—the guests were largely men whose brains create the theatre—the subject was the Theatre.

As playwright after playwright spoke, critic after critic, actor after actor; and as playgoer after playgoer followed them, every mortal of them all took the whole object and function of the drama as being to amuse! That was to be the standard of *its achievement. The horse-laugh was to be lord of all! the snigger and giggle to weave the splendid cloak of its majesty! the titter its title to fame!*

Mark you, these were not the members of a young men's debating society, with down on lip, and with inexperience as their chief foundation to the certainties; these were not the members of a young women's social club, with quaint and pretty egg-shell ideals set like wax-fruit under the glass case of their untried thinking-machinery—but men of established repute in the theatre: some of them men who have made large fortunes and solid names!

It were as though one stood in Bedlam.

Had that novelist arisen and uttered the famous vulgarity that men go to the theatre to experience the thrill of beholding the freely displayed charms of the actresses, and women to gloat upon the actor's calves, he would have seemed in place.

Chapter XXIV

OF THE PROVINCE OF THE ART OF THE DRAMA TO AMUSE

IS the drama of vast importance to the human achievement in our moving forward towards our higher destinies? Is the Art of the Theatre an affair of significance to the life of the people? or is it merely an affair of Amusement? mere farce and tomfoolery, designed to help by side-splitting comicalities in mitigating the boredom of our evenings? the measure of its success the gallons of our laughter?

Upon the answer the theatre depends.

For the Art of the drama is encumbered with this Old Man of the Sea—the widespread idea that the whole aim of the theatre is to amuse, just as the art of painting lies under the blight of the falsity that Art is Beauty.

If the aim and object of the drama be simply to amuse, it would even then have a healthy and sufficient reason for support. Nevertheless, if it be so, then the theatre is doomed. It has against it the

music-hall, and half-way house to the music-hall
that creates music-hall comedy.

These are just as amusing as the theatre—ay, for
the masses, more amusing. Indeed, the players in
them both are as skilled in amusing as are the players of the theatre. Nay, has not genius stepped over
the footlights of the music-hall, often from out
the theatre, and touched with its wondrous flame
the art of Yvette Guilbert, and her like, lifting their
Art to the highest rank of the theatre, and in the
doing uplifting and purifying it?

But—and note this well—the moment that
genius has stepped upon the boards of the music-
hall we get a far higher factor than mere amusement strutting the stage!

Amusement is a healthy, a legitimate, and hu-
manising part of life; but it is not its whole object,
nor its greatest object. By consequence, whilst it
has its proper and right place, and a large place, in
Art—it is not the greatest place. He who has no
gaiety in his heart is a curse here on earth, and let
us sincerely hope, is damned hereafter; for, even if
he stole into heaven, to such as he the blithe splendour of a handsome eternity would be as detestable
a hell as he would have his fellow-mortals to walk

on earth had he a hand in the ordering of things.
Fortunately, the Glum Ones have not the intimate
knowledge of God's Will that they would usurp.

But Amusement is an affair of conditions. Some
would guffaw to see an old lady fall down the stairs
and her wig come off—some at a joke in the comic
press—some at the lack of jest therein—some at
the dull inanities of facetious magistrates—some at
street-urchins who pluck at a drunken woman's
bonnet-strings. Indeed, when we arrive at laughter, we are amongst the incongruities—that which
is quaintness to one man may be a solemn rite to
another. What is comedy to an Oriental may be
tragedy to a Briton; as when Eha found that his
Chinese cook, who kept the kitchen fresh and clean
and speckless, and cooked like a demi-god, washed
his feet in the soup-tureen.

Fortunately, the function of the theatre is not
simply to amuse. It is far more profound and essential a need to a large life.

Tragedy does not amuse.

There are deep emotions in the heart of man that
are not rooted in laughter.

It does not amuse to see the ill-fated Juliet slay
herself for love. The great temptations of life, the

great passions, the sublime moods, pity, tears, self-sacrifice, the agonies of life, heroic aims, mighty endeavour, the majesty of things, the godhood that is in man, the weaknesses that are in him—these are not amusing. These do not arouse the hee-haw —except from asses.

No. The function of the theatre is not to amuse. It is built upon a surer foundation than the guffaw —wrought of more exquisite fabric than from the warp and woof of empty titterings; its satire more vitriolic than the light acids of sarcastic snigger-ings.

Therefore, most fitly, the mightiest dramas of the ages are not given to amusement. *Hamlet* does not amuse, nor *Macbeth*; it is scarcely to be tickled that the playgoer sits through the acts of *Romeo and Juliet*; there is a more vital sense aroused by the comedy of *The School for Scandal* than all its merry laughter.

It is, of course, true that a theatre must be attractive; but is that any reason why vulgarians should browbeat us into the law that it is only to amuse—nay, should put on the strut of morality, and compel their yawning amusement upon us as its supreme function? Art has just as much to do with the ugly and the horrible and pain and death and the agonies and shame and majestic and sublime things as with laughter. Indeed, the Art that makes vile things beautiful or merely amusing, is bad Art. Drunkenness and adultery and jealousy and hate are no subjects for glossing. The vices, made alluring, gain in their allure—'tis a very platitude; yet smug traffickers of the theatre grow rich upon it, and splutter with moral indignation when vice is shown to be a vulgar thing! So quaint is the human!

O Morality! what devildoms are wrought in thy name!

Chapter XXV

OF THE MANIFOLD DANGERS THAT THREATEN THE ART OF THE DRAMA

IT has been neatly said that the Art of the drama must state itself through Conflict of character—that dramatic action is not created unless there be an Obstacle which the heroic element of the drama must assail—that if the heroic element in the drama overcome the obstacle which creates the conflict, the result is Comedy; but if the heroic element fail to overcome the obstacle, the result is Tragedy.

Any element entering into the theatre that is not true to life makes either for the travesty of tragedy called Melodrama, or that travesty of comedy which results in Farce.

Whence it follows that the dangers to true drama as an Art are manifold. There is danger from within and from without. From within, the debasing of its Art by the vile trafficking of its splendours into a sordid and commercial thing—whether the stage-manager make the scenic set-down life falsely, exaggerating this way or that, fail to utter truth; whether the actor debauch the true value of the drama's relation to life in order to gain personal advantage and personal profit; whether the stage-manager make the scenic setting of the theatre overwhelm and thereby destroy the vitality of the drama or otherwise usurp the Art of the drama; or a dozen and one distortions and extravagances of over-statement or understatement. These and other dangers assail the Art from within, and are in full career to-day as always, threatening the significance and majesty of the Art of the theatre. They always will be.

But there is a danger from without of even more serious import to the dignity of the drama than all these vulgarities and deformities; and it is none the less a demoralising influence in that it is exerted against the Art of the theatre by a part of the community that is in its degree largely intelligent; nor is it any the less demoralising in that this part of the community stands aloof from it and shuns it. For, surely, it needs no proof that if the intelligent part of the people stand aloof from the Arts, the Arts must fall into the hands of the baser part. The Arts cannot be blotted out, unless we would live

in the prison of the mad. One of the worst offend-
ers against the Arts is the Puritan.

The very man who beats his breast and thanks
God he never enters the ungodly playhouse is a
corrupter of the Art of the theatre; or who, going
to the theatre, arrayed in outworn ideas and hide-
bound hypocrisies or spectacled with a narrow and
petty vision, resents the utterance of the truth
when that truth is distasteful to him, or howls
down the revelation of the new truth that alone
can urge the race forward to nobler enterprise
and higher endeavour.

And the pathetic part of the sad business is that
it is just this Puritan in us that most deeply de-
plores this state of degradation, which largely
creates that degradation by its enmity to all that is
living and forward-moving in Art—that Puritanism in us, which, if it could but be persuaded to
raise its eyes from the grey unlovely thing that it
so often mistakes for goodness, and could be persuaded to shed the pharisaic cloak of conventional-
ities, would itself the most greatly benefit by
looking at life more in the full.

The Puritan in us has come to paint certain fail-
ings of humanity blacker out of all relation to other

and viler blacknesses which it is smugly content to
see as only grey. Of the false standards of Puritanism what could be more significant than the
meaning it attributes to the very word "Morality"?
When your ordinary man, whether bishop or
butcher or burglar, speaks of Immorality, he ever
means sex irregularity. Yet the irregularities of the
acts of sex are, as often as not, mere rebellion
against the grave and unnatural laws forced upon
men and women by the mere commercial ordering
of society, more by this very Puritanism than by
any other law-making instinct in us. It is the everlasting Thou Shalt Not which is the refrain to our
litanies and commandments, that creates the irregularities of sex. Yet the love of man for woman,
of woman for man, is one of the most urgent needs
of being, one of the most vast and potent instincts,
one of the sanest and noblest incentives to life—
insistent as hunger or thirst. The love of man and
woman, if it go astray from the crude arithmetic
of the statute-book, is often the most forgivable of
all strayings; there is no sin in a woman loving a
man, nor in a man loving a woman—the sin, the
immorality, is in the repudiation of the love. The
law, far less the penalities of the law, cannot make

or unmake that love; it can at best but protect the
commercial consequences; but it can and does
often bind together in that hellish of sins, a loveless
marriage, men and women who not only hold no
love for each other, but loathe each other. The so-
called moral law may thus become the foulest immorality. Worse than this foulness, it is often
compelled upon a man and woman by their fellow-
Puritans, who are at the very time taking that
usury from others so bitterly denounced by the
Christ, to say nothing of their being guilty of acts
of tyranny and swindling and lying and thieving
towards these others, even while they beat their
breasts and thank God for their good morality,
which, when all's said, means only too often that
they love no woman over well!

THE Puritanical prejudice against all the Arts is
dying out as to most of them, but is still violent
against the theatre. This bias against the Arts is
deep-rooted. And, of a truth, just as it has had
sorry ground for growth in the past, so to-day it is
only too often fed by the innuendo and the cyni-
cism of much that is uttered in the theatre—the
censor'd theatre.

Now, this Puritanism cannot be ridden down rough-shod; it is at the back of much that is vital to the race. And this Puritanical bias is not so serious as it might be, since Puritanism has this great saving grace, it has the desire to be intelligent —indeed, the fault of its very virtue is that Puritanism separates the intellect from the emotions, and places it too high above them. But, mark you, for one act that we do owing to the guidance of the intellect, we do a dozen and one at the instinct of our emotions. A great emotion will always ride down a great intellect. The soul of a man has its home in his heart, not in his head. The emotional appeal thrills and rouses to action; the mere reason leaves action cold. Nay, when a man lays down the years that have been leased to him out of the vastness of things, he will surely be accounted a man not by what he has not done, but by what he has done—not by what he has thought or intended, but by what he has endeavoured—not by the laws of life that he has not broken, but by the laws of life that he has accomplished—by the life that he has lived, not by the life that he has shirked.

Now, being intelligent, this Puritanical element has only to be convinced of the value and reality of Art in order to seek it. The Puritan has always regarded the Arts with suspicion because he has wholly misunderstood their function and their true significance—whether Jew or Gentile, Anglican or Catholic, Nonconformist or Agnostic, Mohammedan or Goth. Yet the Puritan has steadily fed upon these very Arts unwittingly; otherwise he must have starved, body and soul. Already he has taken Literature to himself; nay, from the very pulpit is quoted the deep wisdom that Shakespeare uttered from the abhorred stage of the theatre; and from the reading-desk are given forth the sublime fiction of the parables of the Man of Sorrows.

In simple truth, Puritanism not only cannot destroy the Arts; but must itself have walked the madhouse or the desert without their aid. In short, Puritanism but assists by its enmity to demoralise the Arts the moment it leases them to become the plaything of the corrupt and the vile. The cure for the Puritanical bias against the drama is simply to prove the true function of the drama to the national conscience.

No man may treat the Arts with a sneer and be aught but a dullard, and a vicious one.

The question for the Puritan is not whether the

Arts shall be—he has no power to belittle life, even if he have the narrow brain. What he has to decide is whether the Arts shall add to the dignity and the majesty of life, or whether he shall help to make them a thing of the gutter by his disdain.

WHAT he does at present is disastrous. He leaves the theatre to be the ready home for the exposition of vice, if vice be made alluring; whilst the new truths, and vice made hideous, are thrust from the stage. All untruth is vicious.

Chapter XXVI

OF THE PURITAN IN US ALL

WE must first of needs define exactly what is the Puritan in us. Not, be it understood, the Stigginses and the caricatured Kill-joy, but the type of being whom every religious movement tends to produce —the Jews bred him; the Mohammedans; the Mediæval Church; the Reformation; the Agnostic; the Atheist, all bred him—all breed him.

Not only the man who goes about the world insulting his Maker by for ever crying out that the world is a botchy affair and ill-constructed, hinting to his Maker how much better he himself would have arranged the Universe—the long-faced rogue who goes to church or chapel three times on Sunday and sands the sugar during the rest of the week. But the Puritan that lurks in us all—own cousin to the Puritan that, when kept within bounds and at its best, saves us, and has over and over again saved peoples from falling into the trough of excess and wallowing in the debauching of life—the healthy Puritanism in our blood that has taught us to discipline our powers and to curb our baser passions.

The moment that the Puritan that is in us over-balances the humanities—the moment that we indulge the Puritan in us to excess, and allow it to make us into ascetics and afraid to live life, at that moment it becomes itself a vice in us, and a black and ugly vice—as Thrift becomes the most unlovely of the vices if we allow it to pass beyond the threshold of self-discipline into the unbridled habit of the Miser.

The moment that the Puritan in us becomes fearful of the splendour of life, the moment that it makes us mistake the denials of life—the law Thou Shalt Not—to be the Reality of Life, instead of the more majestic law Thou Shalt with Honour (God's law, or wherefore made He us?), from that moment Puritanism becomes a black sickness and an abomination. From that moment the reality of life is warped and distorted, and not the less self-murdered because we set the brass halo of false morality about our skulls. Beware the courage of fearfulness! 'Tis a mean courage!

And one of the surest signs of this black sickness coming to a people is its suspicion of the Arts—

that strange idiot's frenzy that would crush even
the good out of the Arts since evil also may be in
them! As though there were anything good which
may not be made evil. Puritanism, grown fanatical,
would strangle Art altogether, mistrusting others
to use it nobly since it mistakes its own powers to
use it cleanly.

You shall see this Puritanical suspicion of, and
enmity towards, the Arts in the record of every
race. Yet what a crack-brained folly it is!

Mohammedans are forbidden the carving of figures in or on their mosques, forbidden the por-
traiture of men, lest the faithful shall fall to the
worship of images—yet the True Believer flings
away his life in battle, urged to it by the emotional
oratory of his faith; and, where he falls, you shall
ever find about his neck, worn as a little charm to
keep his quaint fantastic soul from harm, sewn
into exquisitely wrought leather work, fragments
of the mighty literature of the Koran! An Art
within an Art!

So the Roundheads, thundering against the Arts
lest they turn men's eyes to graven images, made
the land hideous with sculptures overthrown,
statues mutilated, things of Art destroyed; yet,

even as they did these scandalous and childish things in the Name of the Lord, they listened, with bent heads of reverence, to works of fiction, some amongst the supreme works of Art the world has known—the parables of the Man of Sorrows—and went into battle shouting the Psalms, their nerves thrilling to the music of words wrought by the master-skill of the great Elizabethan translators of the Bible!

Thus we see fanatics, even whilst striving to strangle the Arts, employing the Arts, yet mistrusting their own powers to employ them healthily, not realising that they cannot destroy them, since Art is a necessity of human life. They themselves employ Art—not knowing what they do!

Chapter XXVII

OF THE POWER OF THE DRAMA

IT may be that some of the Arts—music and painting—are difficult to transmit to the crowd unless stated in simple forms, and that they need subtle understanding; but the Art of Oratory goes straight home to most of us. The Orator, being compelled to appeal to an audience, is thereby compelled to keep to the larger methods of his craft. And the Drama, that holds nearly all the other Arts, is so vivid, direct, and compelling, that if an idea be translated into terms of the emotions, and placed upon the stage, how false it rings if it be false, how true if it be true! At once—on the instant—it rings its victory, or sounds its own death-knell.

If the playwright's revelation of life be true, then by and through the players we live the experience of it upon the stage; and it becomes a part of our life for ever. If the revelation be ennobling, we are ennobled—if base, we are debased thereby. If the revelation uplift us, the characters that played before us increase the circle of our acquaintance with the heroes that become our comrades and yield us their good-fellowship.

For no Art compels the imagination and usurps the senses more than the Art of the theatre. The idea, turned by the Art of the playwright into terms of the emotions, reduced from vague thought into living example, poured through the vision and the hearing into our very being, compels the imagination, usurps our sensing. The effect of the drama is prodigious.

Chapter XXVIII

OF THE HOPE OF SALVATION FOR THE PURITAN

NOW, it is not enough to establish this seeming paradox that the Puritan, even whilst he is turning up shocked eyes and flinging up hands of expostulation at the Art of the theatre, is thereby one of the worst and most demoralising enemies to the nobility of the drama. It may seem at first glance that it is impossible to persuade the sickly fellow to take the cure, since he fondly believes himself uncommon well—or, even if suffering self-questionings, he is of the tribe that blasphemously prefers to suffer a plague of boils as the will of the Almighty, rather than take to prettier habits that evade boils, fearing thereby to be thought to question the likelihood of his Maker being particularly interested in sending him a plague of boils, preferring to accept affliction rather than be passed over. But it were madness to seek sense in much of the reason of Puritanism, since the Puritan in us has at times as crude ideas of blasphemy as of morality.

Yet—and here we reach the point of greatest hope, as we also come to the kernel of the strange paradox—*the Puritanical part of the community is to-day, without question, most ambitious to be intelligent*—shows an eager desire to know, to understand. Its initiative is enormous; its power enormous; its influence, for good or ill, enormous. It has as undoubtedly the intention to be honest. It is the class that reads; it is reading solid and significant literature.

It has at heart a desire, if a somewhat fearful desire, to know the truth—and to seek it. But it is afraid to leave achieved and solid ground in order to reach higher—like a child wanting to walk on his hind legs but afraid to leave all-fours. It is so steeped in Thou Shalt Not, that it at once starts in alarm before any hint of Thou Shalt. It is as though a man feared to light a fire to gain warmth for his starved understanding lest he fall into the flames—who therefore cowers in some chill unlit corner of a dingy existence, shivering from dread of burning; it is as though, if one drink of the wine of life, one must stoop to hoggishness. Nay, he has come to look upon this unworthy fearfulness of living life as though it were a virtue, forgetting that to fear to live is as ugly contempt of his body's significance as the wallowing in, and making bankrupt, the splendour of the wondrous miracle that has been granted to him for the using—and of which it is said that he may one day be asked to render an account.

Mighty as are the things of the Intellect, they are small as against the splendid things of the Emotions. To feel the majesty of things, to feel pity, love, friendliness, good-fellowship, disdain, contempt, and the many-faceted Emotions, lifts the splendour of manhood above all the splendours and disdains of the Intellect. We act our nobler selves in response to the emotions rather than in answer to the intellect.

If he could only be persuaded to listen to the mighty significance of Art, he would confess his sin and put foolishness from him.

But how shall his ear be caught?

Chapter XXIX

OF THE GOLDEN GOD OF THE PURITAN
—THRIFT

THE British Puritan, who was aforetime the champion of Free Speech, the enemy of tyrannies, the breaker of Hide-Bound laws, is to-day in power. And being in power, he has in his turn borrowed the tyrant's weapons from the tyrannies that he overthrew, and has learnt to refuse to listen to criticisms of himself—has found the password of the conspiracies to be silence—has come to demanding the subjection of such as do not agree with him.

Let us step aside from the Arts for a moment, and take for instance his attitude towards the nation's courage. To become free he realised that he must wear sword on hip—weapon for weapon—against his oppressors. He has since decided—and rightly decided—that militarism is a bad thing. He has proceeded, as he always does, to extremes; and banns the soldier and the sailor as unclean things—sneers at the men in time of peace who

guard his complacent sleep o' nights and watch his
leisured ease and ring his far frontiers round about
with courage, whilst he, *under their protection,
and through that protection of the man with the
rifle alone,* is free to pursue his daily calling. In his
right and proper hostility to compulsory courage
—courage gone insane—the Puritan dreads to approve of courage sane. Therefore he will not listen
either in words or in print to those who would
speak to him of his voluntary duty to share the
nation's courage.

So likewise with the Arts.

But let us allow for a moment that the Puritan
is right—that just as he is justified in evading his
duty of manhood to share the burden of the courage of his race, justified in deputing it to others to
guard his leisure whilst he is what he calls giving
himself to honourable works, so is he also justified
in giving the cold shoulder of his disdain to the
Arts, and in refusing to listen to the statement of
their significance.

Well; so be it!

*But what does he set up for himself as being of
more value to life than either of these activities?*
Reduced to practice, his chief aim in life is Thrift.

He lives for Thrift—to make money—Success in Business. The man who holds the eyes of the city is he who makes great wealth. The man who makes great wealth pursues wealth with a stubbornness of purpose and a single ambition which are astounding. He pursues the making of wealth before all things; even though he be sometimes generous and charitable to such as he has not ruined or jockeyed or outreached or misused.

Nay. Does he not even write volumes? *"Get On or Get Out."* My godmother, what a book! what a stripping naked of a soul!

Thrift, indulged in with virile restraint and in due degree, is a good and honourable thing. But Thrift become the goal and chief aim of this our little wandering to and fro, before the light goes out, surely becomes the most sordid of all vices, the grey unlovely habit of the miser! It is Thrift gone crazy—as everything he approves is Approval gone crazy—everything he hates, Hate gone crazy.

Follow such a man into his hideous home; corner him in his inmost sanctuary, made fearful with ugly furnishments, or packed like a vast museum with priceless antiquities bought because of their money-value, set against wall-papers that make the

teeth ache—clutch his soul by the throat and shake
the truth from him—dig out the grey matter of
his brain and examine it, and you shall find figures
and prices and percentages thick as microbes in
the nasty mess.

Track him to his unlovely office, where he lives
the greater part of his day, and you shall find him
passing this precious lease of life, that is his for all
too short a while, and shall never again be his,
amidst surroundings and furnishments that are the
dunghill of man's design.

Yet this idea of mere Commerce being the whole
standard of a nation's splendour, how Universal it
is to-day! And this Commerce that is flung at us
as the All and End of national aspiration, and
fabric of a people's grandeur; what has it to do
with Peace or Brotherhood or one's duty towards
one's fellows, or the Nobility of Existence? Are its
Heroes such fine fellows, when all's said? Look at
the nation to-day: what is it torn between, except
those that clamour for mere wealth for the rich as
against those who clamour for a decent life for the
people?

I tell you Commerce is War. From morning until night, War—and a hideous form of War as

often as not. Its very basic principle is to buy from
one man at the lowest price to which you can grind
his poor brain and the labour of his hands, in order
to sell at a higher price to others. Some of the greatest traffickers in industry are men who not only
do not create industry, but who would be hard
put to it to carry on an industry were they driven
to it. What are the awful cruelties and brutalities
of War compared with the infinitely more vast and
brutal wreckage of human lives and hearts and
hopes that are the blood-toll of Commerce? Young
lives ground down, spirits crushed, and bodies
maimed—to make vulgarians vastly rich. Ask the
wives and widows and children of the thousands
slain or mutilated or broken who have fallen during the last ten years on the railways of this country alone—ask the derelicts whose eyes and right
arms have rotted in the potteries to make gold for
others—ask the poor women who stitch and strive
away their grim existence in sweating-dens!

Indeed, for what are Wars waged but for this
very Commerce?

LET the Puritan in us beware of the idols that he
sets above his hearth. For when he stands, at his

life's ending, and yields up the title-deeds of the lease of his adventure upon this earth, it is not the gold for which he has craved that will be his crown; not the number of times that he has ranted that he is a miserable sinner; not the proud sum of the petty tyrannies that he has put upon his neighbours to make them good in his drab reckoning; not the number of grey days that he has compelled upon others; but the use to which he has put the making of the manhood that was in him, the degree to which he has helped his race forward to mastery and the nobilities.

We can pay too high a price for Thrift.

Let Thrift keep its right proportion in our day.

Live your life full—do not rush through a sordid day, threading your way through the vulgarities, to mean goals. Let no man crouch in dark corners fearful of forward-living, lest he fail to reach the heights.

The man who is merely rich in gold may be but a prisoner in a gilded cage, poorer in the splendid Emotions of life than the poorest of the poor. For, that man who accounts himself rich, and has no sympathy with the poor and the suffering about him; who knows naught of the wounds and the sorrows and the hunger and the agonies that vex his race, nor of the aspirations and high hopes that are the beacon-light to his fellow-men, is utterly poor—as he is wholly beneath contempt.

Is it riches to sit within the four walls of a narrow counting-house, day in day out, for seventy years, and know that you but possess gold?

Even the mightiest poet can at best but write a poem; it is the birthright of every man to live one.

They that grub for wealth as an end are like mad swine that bury their eyes in noisome swill, unsuspecting that life is a glorious pageant—and goes by.

Of a truth, just as Thrift or Courage or all good human attributes can be, and are, debauched, so also can the Arts be degraded; but is it therefore reason that they *must* be? Is that therefore reason why a man shall fear the glory of his adventuring through the Arts? Is that reason enough, forsooth, that he shall shrink from increasing his experience in the vast realm of ennobling emotions?

It is as though one feared to eat, lest one fall to gluttony.

Life is a great Thou Shalt—not an enfeebling incubus of belittling Thou Shalt Nots.

There is a poem in which a man so feared to

launch upon the wayfaring of life, dreading the misadventures and dangers which might befall, that he built him a strong castle, and therein sat shivering and alone, fearful of his daily food lest other's hands might poison him, and thus and otherwise set watch and guard against the rest of the world—and the others went sailing over the seas; their ships through devastating tempests came gaily to port; and so they stepped it blithely along the highway of their journey across the earth, loving each lad his lass, and trudging it and fighting and living and dying like men—but *he* was swallowed in an earthquake shock.

'TIS said that Man's Ideal Day should be divided into eight hours of honest toil, eight hours of rest-giving sleep, eight hours of healthy recreation; and surely the Puritan could do worse, and often does worse, than enlarge his heart and brain in the ennobling atmosphere of the Arts! But whether he do so or not, let him make no slightest mistake about it, that if he turn fearfully from the vast wide-ranging emotions of the drama, by that very act he increases the number of its enemies, and but hands the splendid realm of the Art of the theatre to the debauchers of its magnificence—yields its majesty to the impudences of the base of heart.

He has no choice but Yea or Nay.

When Art steps forward and calls for the suffrage of the race he *must* take sides. His approval or his refusal falls one way or the other. It lies with him, quite as much as with us all—for *Art must and will be*—whether the drama shall be a light to lighten the hearts of men, or shall fall and rot, to make the fœtid soil for the growth of the vulgarities.

Chapter XXX

OF THE MIGHT OF THE THEATRE

AND this stately edifice of man's imagination, this splendid realm of Art, the Theatre—do you tell me, in sober seriousness, that it is to be narrowed down to the province of a booth at a fair? a place set up but to tickle the country bumpkins into yaw-haws, or bring spluttering giggles from gilded noodles? a whirligig for the making of laughter? a mere place of amusement? a junket, much like the kicking of a tin can up and down an alley?

Life is made up of far more majestic and wondrous things, far more thrilling things, than laughter.

So therefore is Art.

Men and women go to the theatre, not for amusement, but for the thrill of life—to get away from their narrow day, to live awhile in a wider world, to step into the realm of the higher emotions, to peer at a larger life, and to walk amidst a larger experience. In the theatre, the apprentice may know awhile something of the power and majesty

of kingship over men, be made to feel the awful
dignity of lordship over the world—the princess
may learn to weep and laugh and rejoice with Cin-
derella—the idle rich to share the dignity of the
heroism of the laborious poor. Each man and
woman in the hushed theatre rises for a while out
of self; and, so certainly do the homely virtues
prevail, each man in spirit crosses the footlights
and struts it in the hero's habit, each woman trips
it in the heroine's cloak. The burglar in the gallery
is he who most loudly hisses the villainies. 'Tis the
City cheat and swindler in the stalls who loudest
claps his gloved hands at the cry of "Stop thief!"
For a while even the base reach out to nobility.

The theatre is a great republic where, for a few
hours of an evening, all men are equal; ay, and if
the full truth were known, many a conscience has
awakened in its ranked tiers. No man leaves a
great play without having enlarged his life, and
without having added to his circle of friends the
comradeship of the heroes of the imagination.

And surely it is a splendid thing to be made to
thrill with the high aspirations and the emotional
enthusiasms that make for heroism in man! Surely
it is no ignoble thing to be made to suffer shame

for his shame—to be made to hate what is hateful
—to be overcome with pity for what is pitiful,
with contempt for what is contemptible! Even to
know the remorse that another has known is to
enlarge the heart, to increase the scope of the manhood and the womanhood of the race—to add ter-
ritory to the garden of life. Surely *that* is a hand-
somer life that is the richer for having known lofty
sensations than is the empty frightened entity of
him who crawls timidly along the shadows of a
narrow path to mean goals, whose shrinking from
the splendid adventure of living is the sole aim of
his paltry egoism, whose barren lack of the noblest
emotions of man is his chief source of pride!

Of all the Arts, the most vivid, the most easily
understood, the vastest in its appeal, is the Art of
the theatre. It is the Art in which the English race
stands supreme above the achievement of the ages.
The drama lifts, guides, inspires, greatly influences
—or it degrades. For, in the drama, the problems
of life are made into a felt reality, and are seen in
their due value in the fierce light of the furnace
of truth. There is no virtue in disdaining the theatre. If it fall, it will be usurped by the vulgarities.
There is no half-way house. If the Art of the thea-

tre fail to reach the heights, it will be the fault and act of those within the theatre who debauch its vital functions into a vulgar and sordid traffic, and of those without the theatre who permit the cant and ignorance of the Puritan in us to cut down the tree of life and leave its rotting stump to vileness and putrefaction. And it is the Puritan who will most deeply suffer, by narrowing his wayfaring into a petty crawling, and thereby flinging his breed among the lesser peoples, who fear to live, and dread to feel, who atrophy their strength and render into greyness the godlike miracle of life that has been wasted upon their meagre and self-sufficient souls, who account starvation a morality, and are horrified that God should smile. He who buries his talents in a napkin fitly deserves the eternal curse.

ENVOI

ENVOI

COME! cries the race to Youth as Youth stands hesitant, perplexed before many teachers, upon that day that the gates of his schooling have clanged upon his pupilage:

The hour has struck for song!

Once you have won to the facile hand that creates the craftsmanship at the will's desire, be rid of the squabbles and wrangles of this school and that school; and fearlessly employ every tool of craftsmanship that will create or enhance the impression you would achieve—the which craftsmanship should have been employed from the beginning of pupilage but in the endeavour to create the personal impression. For you the road to fulfilment in the creation of the masterpiece may be lonely and harsh enough. The artist must walk the road of his destiny alone; but the whole vast realm of the sensing is for the conquering, and is fuller life than threading through base mobs. No man may give him aid in revelation. Sincerity of vision

*must be his weapon; fearless truth his whetstone.
The world is a-weary of this eternal tinkering of
antique vessels. Be done with the noise and rattle
of the workshop; get you to the high road of Art.
It leads to the immensities. You have but to reach
out your hand to pluck the splendour. And if
you have not the courage for the heights and a
wide conquest, at least there are pleasant places
by the roadside where fainter hearts may gather
flowers.*

*It is time to burst into song.
We await the singers.
The poet achieves by his song.
Are there singers amongst you?
If so, for the love of Heaven, sing!*

*AND you who have ears for the song, listen to the
true singers!*

*For you the Splendid Wayfaring is your road
to the wider life. For you the way holds no loneli-
nesses, no harsh withdrawals. The quality of the
Arts is in the giving—not in the taking. It is for
you to take. For you the road is strewn with lavish
generosities.*

It is the Arts of our own age that matter. The

rest is an affair of memories—if splendid memories.

If we would make for the heights, we must go forward-gazing.

To the heights, then!

Here ends the book of *The Splendid Wayfaring;* and follows *The Book of Generous Courage.*

Date Due			
Mar 14			